Pray In The Spirit
Spiritual Warfare Prayers That Command Angels

Dr. Yashmira Abi, PhD

Copyright © 2025 Yashmira Abi

All rights reserved. No part of this book may be reproduced, stored in a retrieval system, or transmitted in any form or by any means—electronic, mechanical, photocopying, recording, or otherwise—without the prior written permission of the publisher, except for brief quotations in reviews or articles.

Part I

God's Word Is Alive

Part II

'Lord, Teach Us How To Pray'

Part III

Spiritual Warfare Prayers

    Prayers for Repentance

    Prayers for Overcoming Lust and Temptation

    Prayers for Wisdom

    Prayers for Forgiveness

    Prayers Regarding Healing

    Prayers on Restoration

    Prayers Commanding Angels to Help You

    Prayers Regarding Breaking Soul Ties

    Prayers for Vindication

    Prayers Before Bed

    Prayers to Cancel Bad Dreams

    Prayers for Financial Blessing

Prayers to Break Generational Curses

Prayers to Divorce Spirit Spouses and Anti-Marriage Spirits

Prayers Against Demonic Attacks

Prayers Against Monitoring Spirits

Prayers for Strength and Endurance

Prayers for Binding and Loosing

Prayers for Receiving Joy

Prayers to Bless and Protect Your Home

Prayers to Bless and Protect Your Children

Prayers to Praise and Give Thanks to God

Prayers for Discipline and Self-Control

Special Acknowledgments

Part I
God's Word Is Alive

No other book ever published is like the Bible. It is the live, breathing revelation of God to people, not just an old religious text or a set of moral precepts. Scripture attests to its own vitality by characterizing itself as "living and active" (Hebrews 4:12), with the capacity to change people's hearts, rekindle their minds, and lead them to righteousness. Throughout history the Bible has shaped civilizations, influenced laws, and transformed the lives of individuals who have encountered its power.

The Bible's enduring influence is not due to human effort alone but to its divine nature. As 2 Timothy 3:16-17 states, "All Scripture is breathed out by God and profitable for teaching, for reproof, for correction, and for training in righteousness, that the man of God may be complete, equipped for every good work". This passage affirms that Scripture is not merely a product of human wisdom, but it originates from God Himself. Its divine inspiration makes it living and relevant in every era, speaking across time and cultures to address the deepest needs of the human soul.

The Word of God is living and has the power to transform lives through its enduring nature, its fulfillment in Jesus Christ, and its ongoing relevance through the work of the Holy Spirit.

One of the most powerful descriptions of Scripture is found in Hebrews 4:12:

"For the word of God is living and active, sharper than any two-edged sword, piercing to the division of soul and of spirit, of joints and of marrow, and discerning the thoughts and intentions of the heart." (Hebrews 4:12).

This text emphasizes a number of important facets of the nature of God's Word. First, it is dynamic rather than being a static record, it is a force that communicates to individuals from all generations and in all situations. The Bible consistently discusses the human predicament with extraordinary relevancy, in contrast to human texts that may grow out of date.

Second, the Bible is active meaning that it does not merely inform, but it performs God's work in the lives of those who engage with it. It convicts sinners, comforts the brokenhearted, strengthens the weak, and guides the faithful. When people read Scripture with an open heart, it does not leave them unchanged. From the very beginning of creation, God's Word has been an active force in bringing things into existence. Genesis 1 repeatedly emphasizes that God spoke, and things came to be:

"And God said, 'Let there be light,' and there was light." (Genesis 1:3)

The Word of God is not just informative, it is creative. It has the power to bring life where there was none. This same creative power is at work today. When the gospel is preached, a new spiritual life is created in those who believe. Romans 10:17 affirms:

"So faith comes from hearing, and hearing through the word of Christ."

As people hear and respond to God's Word, they are spiritually reborn, becoming new creations in Christ (2 Corinthians 5:17).

Third, it is piercing and discerning as it goes beyond the surface and reaches the depths of human thoughts, emotions, and motives. It exposes sin, reveals truth, and provides clarity in a confusing world. It is sharper than a two-edged sword, meaning that it has the power to cut through deception and penetrate the deepest recesses of the human heart. Unlike human words, which fade with time, the Bible remains eternal and unchanging. Isaiah 40:8 declares:

"The grass withers, the flower fades, but the word of our God will stand forever".

This verse contrasts the temporary nature of creation with the permanence of Scripture. Cultures shift, philosophies evolve, and human ideas rise and fall, but God's Word remains steadfast. Jesus reaffirmed this truth in Matthew 24:35, saying:

"Heaven and earth will pass away, but my words will not pass away"

Scripture's timeless character attests to its divine authorship. The Bible would have become obsolete over time if it were only the result of human thought. Nevertheless, it remains the most read and disseminated book worldwide, providing direction, insight, and redemption to everyone who seeks it.

The endurance of Scripture is also evident in its preservation. Despite numerous attempts throughout history to destroy or suppress the Bible, whether through persecution, censorship, or skepticism, it remains intact and widely available. Its survival across centuries and continents confirms its divine protection and ongoing relevance.

The Transformative Power of the Word

One of the most compelling pieces of evidence that God's Word is living is its ability to transform lives. Unlike ordinary books, which may inform or entertain, the Bible has the power to radically change a person's heart, mind, and actions.

Paul speaks of this transformation in Romans 12:2:

"Do not be conformed to this world, but be transformed by the renewal of your mind, that by testing you may discern what is the will of God, what is good and acceptable and perfect".

Consistent interaction with Scripture leads to the renewal of the mind, which is the first step toward transformation. The Bible changes people's viewpoints, enables believers to live moral lives, and harmonizes wants with God's will.

Innumerable people have undergone this change throughout history. Through the power of God's Word, many people who were formerly enslaved to sin whether through addiction, hatred, greed, or fear have found new life. Scripture is alive and active, as evidenced by the stories of people who have gone from darkness to light, from despair to faith, and from disobedience to obedience. Psalm 119:105 beautifully illustrates this guiding power: "Your word is a lamp to my feet and a light to my path". Just as a lamp provides illumination in darkness, the Bible offers wisdom and direction in the uncertainties of life. Those who follow its teachings find clarity, peace, and purpose.

While the written Word of God is alive and powerful, its ultimate fulfillment is found in Jesus Christ. The apostle John introduces Jesus as the Word in John 1:1: "In the beginning was the Word, and the Word was with God, and the Word was God." This passage reveals that Jesus is the eternal Word of God, existing before creation and fully divine. John 1:14 further declares:

"And the Word became flesh and dwelt among us, and we have seen his glory, glory as of the only Son from the Father full of grace and truth."

Jesus embodies the Word of God. His life, teachings, death, and resurrection perfectly fulfill the Scriptures, demonstrating their truth and power. He is the ultimate revelation of God's will and character. Those who seek to understand the Word must ultimately look to Christ, for in Him the fullness of God's truth is revealed.

The Role of the Holy Spirit in the Living Word

The Bible is living not only because of its divine inspiration but also because of the active role of the Holy Spirit in illuminating its truth. Jesus promised His disciples that the Holy Spirit would help them understand and apply Scripture:

"But the Helper, the Holy Spirit, whom the Father will send in my name, he will teach you all things and bring to your remembrance all that I have said to you." (John 14:26)

The Holy Spirit continues to guide believers today, helping them comprehend the depths of Scripture and apply it to their lives. Without the Spirit's illumination, the Bible could be seen merely as historical literature, but with His guidance, it becomes a personal and transformative revelation.

This explains why different people can read the same passage and experience unique insights and convictions. The Holy Spirit speaks through Scripture in ways that directly address individual needs, circumstances, and spiritual growth.

The Word of God is living, eternal, and transformative. It is not a passive or outdated text but a powerful force that continues to shape individuals, societies, and history. It penetrates the heart, renews the mind, and directs the steps of those who trust in it. Jesus Christ, the ultimate fulfillment of God's Word, brings it to life through His teachings and sacrifice. As Psalm 19:7-8 declares:

"The law of the Lord is perfect, reviving the soul; the testimony of the Lord is sure, making wise the simple; the precepts of the Lord

are right, rejoicing the heart; the commandment of the Lord is pure, enlightening the eyes."

Engaging with God's Word is not merely an intellectual exercise but a spiritual encounter with the living God. Those who immerse themselves in Scripture will experience its power, truth, and guidance in every aspect of life. Throughout this book, you will learn how to pray in a way that connects you more deeply with God. You will discover the power of prayer to transform your life, to bring peace to your heart, and to strengthen your faith.

Part II
'Lord, Teach Us How To Pray'

A vital part of a believer's life, prayer is a sacred conversation between God and humanity. Another way to become closer to God is via prayer. We are exhorted to "draw near to God, and he will draw near to you" in James 4:8. Believers are reassured by this assurance that God would reply with His presence when they approach Him sincerely. Prayer is a two-way conversation in which God hears us and, in His time and wisdom, answers us with His Word, our circumstances, or a profound sense of peace in our hearts.

Sacred communication with God is not about demanding our desires but aligning ourselves with His purpose. Jesus demonstrated this in His own prayer life, especially in the Garden of Gethsemane before His crucifixion. In Luke 22:42, He prays, "Father, if you are willing, take this cup from me; yet not my will, but yours be done". Jesus models the heart of true prayer by seeking God's will above personal preferences.

In Proverbs 3:5–6, believers are reminded to "Trust in the Lord with all your heart and lean not on your own understanding; in all your ways submit to him, and he will make your paths straight". Prayer is a sacred way to surrender our plans, seeking divine wisdom and direction in every aspect of life.

The Bible offers profound guidance on how to pray emphasizing that prayer should be grounded in faith, humility, and alignment with God's will. One of the foundational aspects of prayer is faith. In the book of Hebrews, we read,

"And without faith it is impossible to please God, because anyone who comes to him must believe that he exists and that he rewards those who earnestly seek him" (Hebrews 11:6).

This verse underscores the importance of trusting in God's existence and His willingness to respond to our earnest prayers. Jesus reinforces this idea in Mark by stating, "Therefore I tell you, whatever you ask for in prayer, believe that you have received it, and it will be yours" (Mark 11:24). Such passages remind us that faith is not merely an accessory to prayer but it's very essence; we are called to approach God with the confidence that He is attentive and generous in answering the sincere pleas of His people.

In tandem with faith, humility is crucial in prayer. The Bible contrasts two approaches to prayer in the parable of the Pharisee and the tax collector found in Luke 18:9–14. The Pharisee, who prided himself on his own righteousness, offered prayers filled with self-exaltation, while the tax collector approached God with a contrite heart, acknowledging his sinfulness by crying, "God, have mercy on me, a sinner" (Luke 18:13). Jesus commended the humble tax collector for his honest repentance, demonstrating that a broken and contrite heart is far more pleasing to God than one steeped in arrogance.

The Hypocrisy of the Pharisees in Prayer

Throughout His ministry, Jesus often confronted the hypocrisy of the Pharisees, particularly in their approach to prayer. While prayer is meant to be a sincere communication with God, the Pharisees used it as a means of self-promotion, seeking attention and admiration rather than true communion with the Lord. Jesus condemned this practice, emphasizing that genuine prayer comes from the heart, not from outward displays of religion.

One of the clearest examples of this is found in Matthew 6:5, where Jesus warns His followers:

"And when you pray, do not be like the hypocrites, for they love to pray standing in the synagogues and on the street corners to be seen by others. Truly I tell you, they have received their reward in full".

Here, Jesus exposes the Pharisees' tendency to use prayer as a performance, designed not to reach God but to gain human recognition. Their long, public prayers were not acts of devotion but displays of spiritual pride. Rather than seeking intimacy with God, they sought applause from people, turning prayer into a spectacle rather than an act of faith.

Another powerful illustration of the Pharisees' hypocrisy in prayer is found in the parable of the Pharisee and the tax collector in Luke 18:9–14. In this story, the Pharisee stands in the temple and prays with arrogance:

"God, I thank you that I am not like other people—robbers, evildoers, adulterers—or even like this tax collector. I fast twice a week and give a tenth of all I get" (Luke 18:11–12).

Instead of humbly seeking God's grace, the Pharisee boasts about his own righteousness, comparing himself favorably to others. In contrast, the tax collector stands at a distance, unwilling even to lift his eyes to heaven, and prays simply: "God, have mercy on me, a sinner" (Luke 18:13). Jesus concludes the parable by stating that the tax collector, not the Pharisee, went home justified before God. This teaching makes it clear that God is not impressed by lengthy, self-righteous prayers but by sincere, humble hearts. Furthermore, in Mark 12:38–40, Jesus issues another strong rebuke:

"Watch out for the teachers of the law. They like to walk around in flowing robes and be greeted with respect in the marketplaces and have the most important seats in the synagogues and the places of honor at banquets. They devour widows' houses and for a show make lengthy prayers. These men will be punished most severely".

Jesus criticizes the Pharisees for exploiting their religious status for personal gain, using long prayers as a facade to mask their corrupt actions. From these passages, it is evident that God values sincerity over eloquence, humility over pride, and a repentant heart over outward displays of piety. True prayer is not about impressing others but about seeking God with an honest and contrite spirit. Jesus teaches that those who pray with humility, like the tax collector, will be exalted, while those who use prayer for self-glorification, like the Pharisees, will ultimately be humbled.

Another critical component of the biblical approach to prayer is seeking God's will. True prayer is not about imposing our desires on God but rather aligning our hearts with His purpose. The apostle John affirms this idea in 1 John 5:14–15:

"This is the confidence we have in approaching God: that if we ask anything according to his will, he hears us. And if we know that he hears us—whatever we ask—we know that we have what we asked of him".

Here, the emphasis is on trusting that God's plans are higher and more perfect than our own, and that prayer is most effective when it resonates with His divine will.

In the Lord's Prayer, recorded in Matthew 6:9–13, Jesus provides not just a collection of words to recite but a comprehensive format that models the ideal posture and priorities of a believer's prayer life. This prayer is structured in a way that guides us through an intimate conversation with God, covering adoration, submission, provision, forgiveness, and deliverance.

First, we begin by addressing God as "Our Father in heaven." This opening is significant because it establishes a relationship based on intimacy and trust. By calling God "Father," we acknowledge His care, authority, and personal interest in our lives. This address also reminds us of the familial bond we share with other believers, emphasizing community and belonging.

Next, the prayer moves to the declaration, "Hallowed be thy name." Here, we express reverence for God's holiness, setting the tone of worship and recognition of His supreme sanctity. This part of the prayer is an affirmation that God's character and nature are above all human affairs, calling us to honor and uphold His reputation in all aspects of our lives.

The prayer then transitions into a plea for the advancement of God's kingdom: "Thy kingdom come, thy will be done on earth as it is in heaven." This section reflects our desire for God's sovereign rule to manifest in our lives and in the world. It is a submission to God's plan, a surrender of our own agendas in favor of His divine purposes. It teaches us that true fulfillment comes when our lives are aligned with His will.

Following this, we ask for our daily needs with the petition, "Give us this day our daily bread." This humble request is a reminder of our reliance on God for every necessity. It expresses gratitude for His ongoing provision and underscores the importance of trusting in His timing and generosity, day by day.

The prayer then addresses the critical issue of forgiveness: "And forgive us our trespasses, as we forgive those who trespass against us." This component of the prayer highlights the reciprocal nature of God's mercy. It teaches us that receiving forgiveness from God is intertwined with our willingness to forgive others. In this way, the prayer calls us to reflect on our own shortcomings and to extend grace and mercy to those who have wronged us.

We end by pleading for direction and defense: "And lead us not into temptation but deliver us from evil." This final prayer recognizes our susceptibility to sin and the existence of spiritual conflict. It is a cry for deliverance from the powers that would harm us as well as a call for spiritual guidance to help us negotiate life's obstacles. We acknowledge our need for God's wisdom and power during difficult times when we seek for His protection.

In conclusion, the Lord's Prayer is a brilliant model that captures the entirety of our connection with God. An intimate speech opens it, followed by worship and submission, an admission of our reliance on divine supply, a request for forgiveness from one another, and a request for God's direction in the face of evil and temptation. By using this structure, believers are encouraged to view prayer as a dynamic, all-encompassing conversation that molds our hearts, harmonizes our desires with God's plan, and strengthens our relationship with Him rather than as a memorization of words.

Part III
Spiritual Warfare Prayers

Please be aware that the prayers in this book may vary in length. Some prayers are shorter and more succinct, while others are longer and more intricate. This variance is deliberate since the length of a prayer does not indicate its efficacy or force. You don't always have to say lengthy prayers. No matter how many or how few words are spoken, God hears and appreciates every prayer. The emphasis is on your relationship with Him, the authenticity of your heart, and the purpose of your words.

Feel free to modify the duration of your prayers to fit your time constraints, current situation, and connection with God. There is no "right" or "wrong" method to pray; it is a personal journey driven by the desire to connect with the One who truly loves you.

Remembering to conclude your prayers in Jesus' name is also crucial. "And I will do whatever you ask in my name, so that the Father may be glorified in the Son," declares Jesus Himself in John 14:13–14. I will fulfill any request you make in my name. When you conclude your prayer in Jesus' name, you are acknowledging His authority and the fact that we can approach the Father via Him.

Prayers for Repentance

Prayer of Confession and Cleansing

Scripture: "If we confess our sins, He is faithful and just to forgive us our sins and to cleanse us from all unrighteousness." 1 John 1:9

Prayer: Heavenly Father, I come before You with a repentant heart, acknowledging my sins and shortcomings. I confess that I have fallen short of Your glory, and I ask for Your mercy and cleansing. Your Word promises that when we confess our sins, You are faithful to forgive and purify us. Wash me clean, Lord, and remove every stain of sin from my life. Renew my spirit and help me walk in holiness. Let the blood of Jesus cover me, and may I be restored to right standing with You. In Jesus' name, Amen.

Prayer for a Contrite Heart

Scripture: "The sacrifices of God are a broken spirit, a broken and a contrite heart—these, O God, You will not despise." Psalm 51:17

Prayer: Father, I humble myself before You and ask for a truly contrite heart. Break every form of pride and stubbornness in me. I surrender my will to You, acknowledging that I need Your mercy and grace. Forgive me for the times I have hardened my heart toward You. I desire to be wholly Yours, with nothing standing between us. Create in me a heart that grieves over sin and delights in Your righteousness. Restore my intimacy with You, Lord, and make me a vessel of Your holiness. In Jesus' name, Amen.

Prayer for Turning Away from Sin

Scripture: "Therefore I will judge you, O house of Israel, everyone according to his ways," says the Lord God. "Repent, and turn from all your transgressions, so that iniquity will not be your ruin." Ezekiel 18:30

Prayer: Father, I repent and turn away from every sin that has entangled me. I renounce anything that has led me away from You. I choose to walk in obedience and reject every temptation that seeks to enslave me. Your Word warns that iniquity can bring destruction, but I choose life in You. Strengthen me, Lord, to resist sin and live righteously. Let my life reflect Your holiness and truth. Give me the grace to walk in newness of life, free from every past bondage. In Jesus' name, amen.

Prayer for Cleansing from Hidden Sins

Scripture: "Who can understand his errors? Cleanse me from secret faults." Psalm 19:12

Prayer: Lord, search my heart and reveal any hidden sin that I may not even recognize. Expose every wrong motive, thought, or action that is displeasing to You. Cleanse me from secret faults and let nothing unholy remain in me. Your Word says that nothing is hidden from Your sight. Shine Your light upon my heart and purify me completely. Let no sin remain unchecked and give me the grace to walk in full obedience to You. In Jesus' name, So be it.

Prayer for Deliverance from Sin's Grip

Scripture: "Therefore do not let sin reign in your mortal body, that you should obey it in its lusts." Romans 6:12

Prayer: Father, I refuse to let sin have dominion over me. I break every stronghold and cycle of sin in my life by the power of Jesus Christ. I surrender my body, mind, and spirit to You, Lord, and ask for the strength to resist temptation. Your Word declares that I am no longer a slave to sin but alive in Christ. I choose righteousness over the flesh, holiness over corruption, and obedience over rebellion. Strengthen me, Holy Spirit, to live in victory over sin every day. In Jesus' name, amen.

Prayer for Repentance from Lukewarmness

Scripture: "So then, because you are lukewarm, and neither cold nor hot, I will vomit you out of My mouth." Revelation 3:16

Prayer: Lord, forgive me for being lukewarm in my faith. I repent for growing complacent and for neglecting my relationship with You. Stir a fire within me, that I may seek You with all my heart, soul, and strength. Remove all spiritual laziness and ignite a passion for Your Word and presence. I choose to pursue You wholeheartedly and to be on fire for Your kingdom. Let my life reflect true devotion and love for You. In Jesus' name, amen.

A Prayer for Breaking Generational Sins

Scripture: "Keeping mercy for thousands, forgiving iniquity and transgression and sin, by no means clearing the guilty, visiting the iniquity of the fathers upon the children and the children's children to the third and the fourth generation." Exodus 34:7

Prayer: Father, I repent for any generational sins that have affected my life and family. I stand in the gap and ask for Your mercy to break every curse and pattern of iniquity. By the blood of Jesus, I cancel every legal right the enemy has to operate in my lineage. Your Word declares that in Christ, I am a new creation, and I refuse to walk in the sins of my ancestors. I loose generational blessings over my family and declare that we will serve the Lord. In Jesus' name, amen.

Prayer for Restoration after Sin

Scripture: "So I will restore to you the years that the swarming locust has eaten." Joel 2:25

Prayer: Lord, I have wasted time and opportunities due to sin, but I believe in Your promise of restoration. I repent for every wasted season, and I ask for Your redeeming power to restore what was lost. Let Your grace cover my past mistakes and lead me into a future filled with hope. Renew my mind, strengthen my spirit, and align my steps with Your perfect will. Fill me with wisdom to discern the paths You set before me and the courage to walk in obedience. I declare that my latter days shall be greater than my former, and that You will use my testimony for Your glory. What the enemy meant for evil, You will turn for my good. Thank You for Your mercy, for Your faithfulness, and for giving me a fresh start. I trust in Your unfailing love and step forward in confidence, knowing You are restoring and redeeming every area of my life. In Jesus' name, amen.

A Prayer for Repentance from Idolatry

Scripture: "Little children, keep yourselves from idols." 1 John 5:21

Prayer: Father, I repent for placing anything or anyone above You in my life. Forgive me for idolatry, whether it be money, relationships, success, or personal desires. I renounce every idol that has taken Your place in my heart. You alone are my God, and I surrender all to You. Help me to seek first Your kingdom and trust in You completely. I cast down every false god in my life and enthrone You as my Lord and King. In Jesus' name, Amen.

A Prayer for a Renewed Mind and Heart

Scripture: "And do not be conformed to this world, but be transformed by the renewing of your mind, that you may prove what is that good and acceptable and perfect will of God." Romans 12:2

Prayer: Lord, I repent for conforming to the ways of the world instead of seeking Your truth. Renew my mind and transform my heart so that I may live according to Your perfect will. Cleanse me from worldly thinking and give me the mind of Christ. I surrender my thoughts, emotions, and desires to You. Let my life be a testimony of Your grace and power. I declare that I am being changed daily into Your image, and I will walk in righteousness. In Jesus' name, amen.

Prayers for Overcoming Temptation

Prayer for a Pure Heart

Scripture: "Create in me a clean heart, O God, and renew a right spirit within me." Psalm 51:10

Prayer: Heavenly Father, I come before You with a heart that longs to be pure. Your Word declares that You can create in me a clean heart and renew a right spirit within me. Lord, I surrender my thoughts, desires, and emotions to You. Cleanse me of all lustful temptations and grant me the strength to resist the enemy's attacks. Fill me with Your Holy Spirit, so my mind is focused on things that are holy and pleasing to You. I reject the lies of the enemy, and I embrace the truth of Your Word. In Jesus' name, Amen.

Prayer to Take Every Thought Captive

Scripture: "We take captive every thought to make it obedient to Christ." 2 Corinthians 10:5

Prayer: Lord Jesus, I acknowledge that lust begins in my mind, and I ask for Your divine power to take every thought captive to make it obedient to You. Help me to reject every impure and lustful thought the moment it enters my mind. Strengthen me to meditate on what is pure, lovely, and of good report. I declare that I have the mind of Christ, and I reject all sinful desires. Holy Spirit, lead me into truth and renew my mind daily. In Jesus' name, Amen.

Prayer for Deliverance from the Flesh

Scripture: "Walk by the Spirit, and you will not gratify the desires of the flesh." Galatians 5:16

Prayer: Father, Your Word instructs me to walk by the Spirit so that I will not gratify the desires of the flesh. I submit myself completely to You, Lord, and I ask that Your Spirit guide me away from temptation. Strengthen my inner man so that I do not fall into the enemy's trap. Let my heart and mind be filled with Your love and truth so that I desire You above all else. I declare that I am dead to sin and alive in Christ. In Jesus' name, Amen.

Prayer for Strength Against Temptation

Scripture: "No temptation has overtaken you except what is common to mankind. And God is faithful; He will not let you be tempted beyond what you can bear." 1 Corinthians 10:13

Prayer: Lord God, I praise You for Your faithfulness. You promised that no temptation would be too strong for me to bear, and that You will always provide a way out. Strengthen me to resist lust and to choose righteousness instead. Help me recognize the escape routes You provide so that I may flee from temptation. I declare that I am more than a conqueror through Christ Jesus. In Jesus' name, Amen.

Prayer to Flee from Lustful Desires

Scripture: "Flee from sexual immorality. Every other sin a person commits is outside the body, but the sexually immoral person sins against his own body." 1 Corinthians 6:18

Prayer: Father, I recognize the danger of lust and sexual immorality, and I choose to flee from it. Give me the wisdom and strength to remove myself from any situation, thought, or influence that leads to sin. Let my body be a temple of the Holy Spirit, set apart for Your glory. I break every agreement with sin and align myself with Your righteousness. I declare that I belong to You, and my life is dedicated to holiness. In Jesus' name, Amen.

Prayer for Renewal of the Mind

Scripture: "Do not be conformed to this world but be transformed by the renewal of your mind." Romans 12:2

Prayer: Lord, I surrender my mind to You and ask for a complete transformation. Let Your Word renew my thoughts and purify my desires. I reject the influence of this world and its corrupt patterns. Holy Spirit, fill me with wisdom and discernment so that I may desire only what is good and pleasing to You. Thank You for empowering me to live a life of holiness and purity. In Jesus' name, Amen.

Prayer for Guarding My Eyes and Heart

Scripture: "I have made a covenant with my eyes not to look lustfully at a young woman." Job 31:1

Prayer: Father, like Job, I make a covenant with my eyes not to look upon anything that leads me into temptation. Strengthen me to turn away from anything that stirs up lust within me. Protect my heart and keep me focused on You. Give me the discipline to avoid sinful media, images, and conversations that do not glorify You. I commit to walking in purity and honoring You in all I see, say, and do. In Jesus' name, Amen.

Prayer for Self-Control

Scripture: "For God gave us a spirit not of fear but of power and love and self-control." 2 Timothy 1:7

Prayer: Heavenly Father, I thank You for giving me a spirit of self-control. For You have not given me a spirit of fear, but of power, love, and a sound mind (2 Timothy 1:7). Help me exercise this gift in every area of my life, especially in overcoming lustful desires. Fill me with Your strength to resist temptation and to walk in the power of Your Spirit. Let fear and weakness have no hold over me, for I am empowered by Your love and guided by Your wisdom. I reject the flesh and choose to live in the victory You have given me through Christ. May my thoughts, actions, and desires be aligned with Your holiness so that my life brings glory to You. Keep my heart steadfast, my mind renewed, and my spirit anchored in Your truth. In Jesus' name, Amen.

Prayer to Find Satisfaction in God

Scripture: "You make known to me the path of life; in Your presence, there is fullness of joy; at Your right hand are pleasures forevermore." Psalm 16:11

Prayer: Lord, I acknowledge that true satisfaction comes only from You. Help me to seek fulfillment in Your presence rather than in fleeting worldly desires. You have made known to me the path of life; in Your presence, there is fullness of joy, and at Your right hand are pleasures forevermore. Fill my heart with joy and contentment in You alone. Let me hunger and thirst for righteousness instead of sinful pleasures. I fix my eyes on You, the author and perfecter of my faith. In Jesus' name, Amen.

Prayer for Accountability and Community

Scripture: "Therefore confess your sins to each other and pray for each other so that you may be healed." James 5:16

Prayer: Father, I recognize the power of accountability in my walk with You. Help me to surround myself with godly believers who will encourage me, pray for me, and hold me accountable. Give me the humility to confess my struggles and seek support when needed. Let my relationships be a source of strength and encouragement as I pursue holiness. I thank You for the community of believers who walk this journey with me. In Jesus' name, Amen.

Prayers for Wisdom

Prayer for Divine Wisdom

Scripture: "If any of you lacks wisdom, you should ask God, who gives generously to all without finding fault, and it will be given to you." James 1:5

Prayer: Heavenly Father, I come before You, acknowledging my need for divine wisdom. Your Word says that if I lack wisdom, I should ask, and You will give it generously without finding fault (James 1:5). Lord, I ask for wisdom to discern right from wrong, to make decisions that align with Your will, and to walk in understanding. Fill my heart with the knowledge of Your truth so that I may navigate life's challenges with clarity and faith. Let Your wisdom guide my steps, guard my tongue, and shape my thoughts. Protect me from the snares of the enemy and from leaning on my own understanding. Help me to trust in You fully, seeking Your counsel in every decision, great or small. May my life be a testimony of the wisdom that comes from above—pure, peace-loving, gentle, and full of mercy. Thank You for Your unfailing guidance and for the assurance that You will never leave me without direction. In Jesus' name, Amen.

Prayer for Wisdom to Overcome the Enemy

Scripture: "Put on the full armor of God, so that you can take your stand against the devil's schemes." Ephesians 6:11

Prayer: Father, the enemy seeks to deceive me, but I put on the full armor of God so that I may stand against the schemes of the devil (Ephesians 6:11). Clothe me with the belt of truth, the breastplate of righteousness, the shoes of the gospel of peace, the shield of faith, the helmet of salvation, and the sword of the Spirit, which is Your Word. Grant me discernment to recognize the enemy's lies and the strength to stand firm against his attacks. Help me to navigate every battle with the wisdom that comes from You, knowing that my fight is not against flesh and blood but against spiritual forces of darkness. Let my mind be filled with divine understanding so that I do not fall into the traps set before me. Strengthen my faith, sharpen my spirit, and teach me to rely fully on You. May I walk in victory, clothed in Your power and covered by Your grace. In Jesus' name, Amen.

Prayer for Wisdom to Speak with Grace

Scripture: "Let your conversation be always full of grace, seasoned with salt, so that you may know how to answer everyone." Colossians 4:6

Prayer: Lord, I ask for wisdom in my words. May my speech always be full of grace, seasoned with the salt of your truth. Give me wisdom to speak life instead of death, to bring encouragement rather than discouragement, and to respond with wisdom instead of foolishness. Let my words be a weapon against the enemy's lies and a source of healing to those around me. In Jesus' name, Amen.

Prayer for Wisdom to Make Right Decisions

Scripture: "Trust in the Lord with all your heart and lean not on your own understanding; in all your ways submit to him, and he will make your paths straight." Proverbs 3:5-6

Prayer: Lord, I acknowledge that my own understanding is limited. I ask for Your wisdom to guide my decisions. Help me to trust You fully and not to lean on my own thoughts or emotions. Direct my path, Lord, and lead me in the way that aligns with Your perfect will. Remove any confusion and replace it with clarity that comes from You. In Jesus' name, Amen.

Prayer for Wisdom to Avoid Deception

Scripture: "Jesus answered: 'Watch out that no one deceives you.'" Matthew 24:4

Father, in a world full of deception, I ask for wisdom to discern truth from lies. The enemy seeks to confuse and mislead, but I rely on Your wisdom to guide me. Open my eyes to see through deception and guard my heart against false teachings and misleading spirits. Let Your truth be my foundation so that I may not be swayed by anything that contradicts Your Word. In Jesus' name, Amen.

Prayer for Wisdom in Spiritual Battles

Scripture: "The weapons we fight with are not the weapons of the world. On the contrary, they have divine power to demolish strongholds." 2 Corinthians 10:4-5

Prayer: Lord, I acknowledge that my battles are not physical but spiritual. I ask for divine wisdom to use the weapons You have given me—prayer, fasting, and Your Word—to defeat the enemy. Give me strategic insight into spiritual warfare so that I may overcome every stronghold that stands against me. Strengthen me with the wisdom to fight with faith and not fear. In Jesus' name, Amen.

Prayer for Wisdom in Relationships

Scripture: "Walk with the wise and become wise, for a companion of fools suffers harm." Proverbs 13:20

Prayer: Lord, help me to choose my relationships wisely. Give me discernment to surround myself with godly influences and avoid those who may lead me astray. Let my friendships be filled with wisdom, encouragement, and truth. Help me to be a source of wisdom to others as well. In Jesus' name, Amen.

Prayer for Wisdom to Resist Temptation

Scripture: "No temptation has overtaken you except what is common to mankind. And God is faithful; he will not let you be tempted beyond what you can bear." 1 Corinthians 10:13

Prayer: Lord, I come before You, recognizing that I cannot walk in victory on my own. I humbly ask You to grant me the wisdom and discernment to recognize temptation before it entangles me. Your Word says in James 1:5, "If any of you lacks wisdom, let him ask of God, who gives to all liberally and without reproach, and it will be given to him." I ask You for the wisdom to identify the subtle tactics of the enemy and the strength to avoid the traps that seek to derail my walk with You.

Father, I acknowledge that the enemy roams like a roaring lion, seeking whom he may devour (1 Peter 5:8), but I stand firm in Your truth. I ask that You strengthen me in my inner being so that I may resist the lures of sin and walk in the fullness of Your righteousness. When temptation comes, give me the courage to stand firm, to choose righteousness over sin, and to honor You with my thoughts, actions, and decisions. Let Your Word be my light and my guide, as Psalm 119:105 says, "Your word is a lamp to my feet and a light to my path." May it illuminate the path of holiness, and may I treasure Your commandments in my heart, that I might not sin against You . Help me to live by Your Word daily, meditating on it, and allowing it to transform me from the inside out. Lord, I know that in my own strength, I am weak, but I rely on Your power.

I pray that the Holy Spirit will empower me to resist temptation, to choose holiness, and to reflect Your love and purity in everything I do. May I honor You with every decision and become more like Christ in my thoughts and actions. Thank You, Lord, for Your faithfulness, Your protection, and Your grace. I trust that You will keep me strong and faithful in this journey of righteousness. I give You all the glory and praise, knowing that in You, I have the victory. In Jesus' name, Amen.

Prayer for Wisdom to Understand God's Word

Scripture: "The unfolding of your words gives light; it gives understanding to the simple." Psalm 119:130

Prayer: Lord, I desire to understand Your Word deeply. For Your Word says, "The unfolding of Your words gives light; it gives understanding to the simple" (Psalm 119:130). Open my mind and heart to receive divine revelation as I read Scripture. Let Your truth illuminate my path, dispelling confusion and darkness, and transforming my mind with Your wisdom. Help me not only to read but to meditate on Your Word day and night, that it may take root in my heart and bear fruit in my life. Teach me to apply Your truth in every situation, that I may walk in obedience and discernment. Let my life reflect the power and clarity that come from Your divine instruction. May Your Word be a lamp to my feet and a light to my path, guiding me closer to You each day. In Jesus' name, Amen.

Prayer for Wisdom to Fulfill My Purpose

Scripture: "Be very careful, then, how you live—not as unwise but as wise, making the most of every opportunity, because the days are evil." Ephesians 5:15-16

Prayer: Father, I do not want to waste the opportunities You have given me. Your Word instructs me to "be careful how I walk, not as unwise but as wise, making the most of every opportunity because the days are evil" (Ephesians 5:15-16). Fill me with wisdom to walk in my calling and fulfill my purpose. Help me to use my time wisely, being intentional with every moment and seeking to glorify You in all that I do. Guard my heart against distractions that pull me away from Your will. Teach me to prioritize what truly matters, to seek first Your kingdom, and to walk in obedience. Strengthen me to be diligent, steadfast, and faithful, redeeming the time You have given me for Your glory. Let my life be a reflection of Your wisdom and grace, and may I impact those around me with the light of Christ. In Jesus' name, Amen.

Prayer for Wisdom in Times of Uncertainty

Scripture: "Whether you turn to the right or to the left, your ears will hear a voice behind you, saying, 'This is the way; walk in it.'" Isaiah 30:21

Prayer: Lord, in moments of uncertainty, I seek Your wisdom. Speak to me clearly and show me the path I should take. Let me not be led by fear or confusion, but by Your voice of truth. In Jesus' name, Amen.

Prayer for Wisdom to Be a Light in Darkness

Scripture: "Let your light shine before others, that they may see your good deeds and glorify your Father in heaven." Matthew 5:16

Prayer: Father, give me wisdom to shine Your light in a world filled with darkness. As Your Word says, "Let your light shine before others, that they may see your good deeds and glorify your Father in heaven" (Matthew 5:16). Let my actions and words reflect Your truth and love so that others may be drawn to You. Use me as an instrument of wisdom and grace, that my life may testify to Your goodness. Help me to be a beacon of hope, kindness, and righteousness, standing firm in faith amidst the darkness. May everything I do point others to Your glory, and may my life be a reflection of Christ's love. In Jesus' name, Amen.

Prayer for Wisdom to Navigate Conflict

Scripture: "But the wisdom that comes from heaven is first of all pure; then peace-loving, considerate, submissive, full of mercy and good fruit, impartial and sincere." James 3:17

Prayer: Heavenly Father, You are the God of peace, and You call me to walk in wisdom in every situation, including conflicts. Lord, I ask for divine wisdom to handle disagreements with grace and love. Let my heart be filled with patience and understanding rather than anger and resentment. Teach me to listen before speaking and to seek reconciliation instead of division. Your Word says that wisdom from above is pure, peace-loving, and full of mercy. I pray that my responses to others reflect these qualities. Remove any bitterness or pride from my heart that would hinder me from seeking peace. Help me to see others through Your eyes and to extend forgiveness as You have forgiven me. When the enemy tries to stir up strife, grant me the wisdom to respond with gentleness and humility. In Jesus' name, Amen.

Prayer for Wisdom in Financial Decisions

Scripture: "The plans of the diligent lead to profit as surely as haste leads to poverty." Proverbs 21:5

Prayer: Lord, You are my provider, and I trust in Your wisdom to guide me in my financial decisions. In a world that promotes greed and recklessness, I ask for wisdom to steward my finances in a way that honors You. Help me to be diligent and disciplined, making choices that lead to stability and not impulsiveness that leads to loss. Father, I reject the spirit of financial lack and mismanagement. Give me the wisdom to live within my means, save diligently, and give generously. Your Word says that the borrower is a slave to the lender, so I pray for wisdom to make choices that free me from unnecessary debt. Teach me to be content with what I have while trusting You for greater blessings. Open doors of financial opportunities that align with Your will, and let my resources be used for Your glory. In Jesus' name, Amen.

Prayer for Wisdom to Guard My Heart and Mind

Scripture: "And the peace of God, which transcends all understanding, will guard your hearts and your minds in Christ Jesus." Philippians 4:7

Prayer: Father, my heart and mind are battlefields where the enemy seeks to plant lies, fear, and discouragement. But I take refuge in Your wisdom, knowing that Your peace will guard me. I pray for wisdom to discern the thoughts I allow into my mind and the emotions I harbor in my heart. Let me not be led by feelings but by Your unchanging truth. Help me to recognize and reject every lie of the enemy. When anxious thoughts arise, give me wisdom to combat them with Your promises. When bitterness tries to take root, remind me to release it through forgiveness. I take captive every thought and make it obedient to Christ. Let Your wisdom be my shield and guide as I walk in mental and emotional stability. In Jesus' name, Amen.

Prayer for Wisdom to Train My Children in Righteousness

Scripture: "Start children off on the way they should go, and even when they are old they will not turn from it." Proverbs 22:6

Prayer: Lord, raising children in a world filled with darkness and deception is a great responsibility. I need Your wisdom every day to guide them in truth and righteousness. Help me to teach them Your ways, not just through words but through my actions. Let my life be an example of faith, love, and integrity. Give me wisdom to discipline with love and correction without anger. Help me to discern their struggles and provide the encouragement they need. Protect them from worldly influences that seek to draw them away from You. Surround them with godly mentors and friends who will reinforce the values of Your Word. Lord, I commit them into Your hands, trusting that the seeds of faith I plant will bear fruit in their lives. In Jesus' name, Amen.

Prayer for Wisdom to Use My Words Wisely

Scripture: "A gentle answer turns away wrath, but a harsh word stirs up anger." Proverbs 15:1

Prayer: Lord, my tongue has the power to build up or tear down, and I desire for my words to bring life. Give me the wisdom to speak with gentleness, kindness, and truth. Help me to know when to speak and when to remain silent. May my words be a source of encouragement, wisdom, and grace to those around me. Remove from me any tendency to gossip, complain, or speak negatively. Instead, let my speech be filled with faith, love, and wisdom. Let me not react impulsively but respond thoughtfully, with words that glorify You. Guard my lips from speaking words that dishonor You or harm others. In Jesus' name, Amen.

Prayer for Wisdom to Walk in Humility

Scripture: "When pride comes, then comes disgrace, but with humility comes wisdom." Proverbs 11:2

Prayer: Father, pride is a dangerous trap that can lead me away from You. I ask for wisdom to walk in humility, recognizing that all I have comes from You. Let me not seek my own glory but to honor You in all that I do. Teach me to be quick to listen, slow to speak, and slow to become angry. Help me to humble myself before You and before others. Let me not be wise in my own eyes, but always seek Your counsel in all things. Keep me from comparing myself to others or seeking validation from the world. Instead, let me find my worth and confidence in You alone. In Jesus' name, Amen.

Prayer for Wisdom to Resist Fear and Anxiety

Scripture: "For the Spirit God gave us does not make us timid, but gives us power, love and self-discipline." 2 Timothy 1:7

Prayer: Lord, fear and anxiety try to overwhelm me, but I stand on Your promise that You have given me a spirit of power, love, and a sound mind. Grant me wisdom to recognize when fear is trying to control me and replace it with faith. Help me to trust in Your sovereignty over my life and not be shaken by circumstances. When worries arise, let me turn to You in prayer instead of dwelling on the unknown. Give me the wisdom to focus on what is true, noble, and praiseworthy. Strengthen me to cast my cares upon You, knowing that You care for me. Let my heart be steadfast, trusting in Your perfect will. In Jesus' name, Amen.

Prayer for Wisdom to Recognize Divine Opportunities

Scripture: "Be wise in the way you act toward outsiders; make the most of every opportunity." Colossians 4:5

Prayer: Lord, You place opportunities before me everyday opportunities to serve, to witness, to grow, and to bless others. I ask for wisdom to recognize these moments and act upon them. Let me not be distracted by the busyness of life but be attentive to the doors You open before me. Help me to walk in discernment, knowing when to step forward and when to wait. Let me not operate in fear or hesitation but with boldness and faith. Use me to impact lives for Your kingdom, making the most of every divine appointment. In Jesus' name, Amen.

Prayers for Forgiveness

Prayer for God's Mercy and Cleansing

Scripture: "Have mercy on me, O God, according to Your unfailing love; according to Your great compassion blot out my transgressions. Wash away all my iniquity and cleanse me from my sin." Psalm 51:1-2

Prayer: Heavenly Father, I come before You with a heart that longs for Your mercy. I have sinned against You, and I acknowledge my need for Your cleansing. Your love is unfailing, and Your compassion knows no bounds. Lord, I ask You to blot out my transgressions and wash away all my iniquities (Psalm 51:1-2). Remove every impurity that separates me from You. I reject the lies of the enemy that tell me I am unworthy of Your forgiveness. Your Word declares that You cleanse those who come to You with a repentant heart. Create in me a clean heart, O God, and renew a steadfast spirit within me. I surrender my past mistakes, my guilt, and my shame to You. Thank You for Your mercy, Lord. Thank You for the blood of Jesus that washes me white as snow. I receive Your forgiveness and stand in the righteousness of Christ. In Jesus' name, Amen.

Prayer to Overcome Guilt and Condemnation

Scripture: "As far as the east is from the west, so far has He removed our transgressions from us." Psalm 103:12

Prayer: Lord, I thank You that Your forgiveness is not temporary, nor is it partial. When You forgive, You remove my sins as far as the east is from the west. Yet, the enemy seeks to bring guilt and condemnation upon me. He whispers lies, telling me that I am beyond redemption. But I choose to stand on Your Word, which declares that I am forgiven. I refuse to live in shame over sins that You have already removed. Your love is greater than my failures, and Your mercy is deeper than my mistakes. I silence every accusing voice of the enemy with the truth of Your Word. I declare that I am a new creation in Christ, and the old has passed away. Lord, let my heart be at peace, knowing that I am fully restored to You. Thank You for the power of Your forgiveness. In Jesus' name, Amen.

Prayer for Strength to Forgive Others

Scripture: "For if you forgive other people when they sin against you, your heavenly Father will also forgive you." Matthew 6:14

Prayer: Father, I desire to walk in the fullness of Your forgiveness, but I know that means I must also forgive those who have wronged me. I confess that at times, my heart resists forgiveness. The pain others have caused me feels too great, and my flesh wants to hold on to resentment. But Lord, I do not want anything to stand in the way of my relationship with You. Your Word commands me to forgive as I have been forgiven. So, right now, I surrender my hurt to You. I release every grudge, every bitter thought, and every memory that seeks to keep me bound in unforgiveness. Holy Spirit, help me to let go completely. Heal the wounds in my heart and fill me with Your peace. Let Your love flow through me so that I may extend grace to others just as You have extended grace to me. I choose forgiveness today, and I will choose it again tomorrow. Thank You, Lord, for setting me free. In Jesus' name, Amen.

Prayer for Restoration and Renewal

Scripture: "Therefore, if anyone is in Christ, he is a new creation. The old has passed away; behold, the new has come." 2 Corinthians 5:17

Prayer: Lord Jesus, I thank You that through Your sacrifice, I am made new. My sins do not define me, for You have made me a new creation. Yet, at times, I struggle to let go of my past. The enemy reminds me of my failures, and I sometimes believe the lie that I am still broken. But Your Word says that the old has passed away, and the new has come. Lord, let that truth sink deep into my heart. I surrender my past, my regrets, and my mistakes to You. Restore me, O God. Renew my spirit and transform my mind. Let me walk in the newness of life that You have promised. I refuse to be bound by yesterday's sins when You have given me a future filled with hope. Thank You for the restoration You bring. I embrace my new identity in Christ, and I move forward in Your grace. In Jesus' name, Amen.

Prayer for Breaking the Chains of Shame

Scripture: "Instead of your shame, you will receive a double portion, and instead of disgrace, you will rejoice in your inheritance." Isaiah 61:7

Prayer: Father, shame has tried to keep me in bondage. It whispers that I am not worthy of Your love, that my sins are too great to be forgotten. But Your Word declares that instead of shame, I will receive a double portion of blessing. Instead of disgrace, I will rejoice in my inheritance. Lord, I break every chain of shame in my life right now. I reject every lie of the enemy that says I must carry the weight of my past. Your forgiveness has covered me, and I am no longer a prisoner to guilt. I receive Your love, Your joy, and Your peace. Let my life be a testimony of Your redemption. In Jesus' name, Amen.

Prayer for Deliverance from the Accuser

Scripture: "They triumphed over him by the blood of the Lamb and by the word of their testimony." Revelation 12:11

Prayer: Lord, the enemy comes against me as the accuser, seeking to remind me of my sins and failures. But I overcome him by the blood of the Lamb and the word of my testimony. I stand on the truth that I am forgiven, redeemed, and set free. No accusation can stand against me because I am covered by Your grace. I silence every voice of condemnation and declare that I am victorious in Christ. Thank You, Jesus, for fighting my battles. In Your mighty name, Amen.

Prayer for a Heart That Reflects Christ

Scripture: "Be kind and compassionate to one another, forgiving each other, just as in Christ God forgave you." Ephesians 4:32

Prayer: Father, I desire a heart that mirrors Yours—a heart full of love, compassion, and forgiveness. Your Word instructs me to be kind and compassionate, forgiving others just as You have forgiven me in Christ (Ephesians 4:32). Lord, help me to let go of anger, resentment, and any bitterness that seeks to take root in my heart. Teach me to be quick to forgive and slow to take offense, just as You are patient and merciful with me. Fill me with the strength to love even when it is difficult, to extend grace even when it is undeserved, and to reflect Your kindness in my words and actions. Shape me into a vessel of grace, Lord, so that I may be an instrument of reconciliation and a light in a world that so desperately needs Your love. May my life testify to the power of forgiveness and the freedom found in Your mercy. In Jesus' name, Amen.

Prayer for Healing Through Forgiveness

Scripture: "He heals the brokenhearted and binds up their wounds." Psalm 147:3

Prayer: Lord, I know that true healing comes when I release the pain of the past. I surrender every wound, every offense, and every betrayal to You. Heal my heart and make me whole again. In Jesus' name, Amen.

Prayer for Victory Over Bitterness

Scripture: "See to it that no one falls short of the grace of God and that no bitter root grows up to cause trouble and defile many." Hebrews 12:15

Prayer: Heavenly Father, I come before You, surrendering the bitterness in my heart. Your Word warns that no bitter root should grow and cause trouble or defile many (Hebrews 12:15). Lord, help me to release any resentment, anger, or unforgiveness that lingers within me. Fill me with Your grace so that I may extend it to others just as You have graciously forgiven me. Soften my heart, Lord, and cleanse me from any thoughts or emotions that hinder my walk with You. Replace bitterness with love, peace, and compassion. Teach me to see others through Your eyes, to forgive as You forgive, and to walk in the freedom that comes from letting go. May my heart be pure and my spirit be filled with Your joy. In Jesus' name, Amen.

Prayer for a Life of Grace

Scripture: "Freely you have received; freely give." Matthew 10:8

Prayer: Lord, as You have freely given me grace, help me to freely extend it to others. Your Word reminds me, "Freely you have received; freely give" (Matthew 10:8). Let my heart be open to giving without hesitation—whether it be love, kindness, forgiveness, or generosity.

Help me to reflect Your boundless mercy in my words, actions, and attitudes. Teach me to serve others selflessly, to love unconditionally, and to give without expecting anything in return. May my life be a testament to the generosity of Your Spirit, and may I always remember that all I have comes from You. In Jesus' name, Amen.

Prayer for God's Mercy and Cleansing

Scripture: "If we confess our sins, He is faithful and just to forgive us our sins and to cleanse us from all unrighteousness." 1 John 1:9

Prayer: Heavenly Father, I come before You in humility, confessing my sins and shortcomings. Your Word assures me that You are faithful and just to forgive when I repent. Wash me clean, Lord, and remove every stain of unrighteousness from my life. Let Your mercy flow over me, renewing my heart and restoring my spirit. I reject every accusation of the enemy, for I stand on the promise of Your forgiveness. Thank You, Lord, for Your grace that covers me. In Jesus' name, Amen.

Prayer to Overcome Guilt and Condemnation

Scripture: "There is therefore now no condemnation for those who are in Christ Jesus." Romans 8:1

Prayer: Lord Jesus, I thank You that in You, there is no condemnation. The enemy seeks to burden me with guilt and shame, but I reject his lies. I accept Your forgiveness and embrace the freedom You have given me. Help me to walk in the confidence of Your love, knowing that my past is covered by Your blood. Strengthen my heart so I may live in the righteousness You have provided. In Jesus' name, Amen.

Prayer for a Forgiving Heart

Scripture: "Bear with each other and forgive one another if any of you has a grievance against someone. Forgive as the Lord forgave you." Colossians 3:13

Prayer: Father, as You have forgiven me, I choose to forgive others. Help me release all bitterness, anger, and resentment that may be hiding in my heart. Teach me to love as You love and to extend grace as You have extended it to me. I refuse to let unforgiveness hinder my walk with You. Holy Spirit, empower me to forgive completely and to let go of every offense. In Jesus' name, Amen.

Prayer for Restoration After Sin

Scripture: "Restore to me the joy of Your salvation and uphold me with a willing spirit." Psalm 51:12

Prayer: Lord, I feel the weight of my sins, but I come to You seeking restoration. Your Word declares that You can renew the joy of my salvation. Lift me out of my brokenness, O God, and fill me again with Your presence. Let me not dwell on my past mistakes but move forward in the grace and purpose You have for me. Strengthen my spirit to walk in obedience and faith. In Jesus' name, Amen.

Prayer to Resist the Enemy's Accusations

Scripture: "For the accuser of our brothers and sisters, who accuses them before our God day and night, has been hurled down." Revelation 12:10

Prayer: Mighty God, I know the enemy seeks to accuse me and remind me of my failures, but I stand on Your Word. Satan has been defeated, and his accusations hold no power over me. I rebuke every voice that speaks condemnation and declare that I am washed in the blood of Jesus. I am no longer bound by my past, for I am a new creation in Christ. Thank You, Lord, for setting me free. In Jesus' name, Amen.

Prayer for a Heart Like Christ's

Scripture: "Be kind and compassionate to one another, forgiving each other, just as in Christ God forgave you." Ephesians 4:32

Prayer: Lord, I desire to reflect Your heart of compassion and forgiveness. Help me to see others through Your eyes, even those who have wronged me. Remove any hardness from my heart and replace it with Your love. I choose to walk in kindness and grace, forgiving as You have forgiven me. Let my life be a testimony of Your mercy. In Jesus' name, Amen.

Prayer to Break Generational Curses of Unforgiveness

Scripture: "The Lord is slow to anger, abounding in love and forgiving sin and rebellion." Numbers 14:18

Prayer: Father, I recognize that unforgiveness can be passed down through generations, but today I break that cycle in Jesus' name. I declare that my family will be known for love, mercy, and reconciliation. Let Your abounding love flow through me, breaking every stronghold of bitterness and resentment. I release every past hurt and embrace the freedom of Your forgiveness. In Jesus' name, Amen.

Prayer for Freedom from Shame

Scripture: "Those who look to Him are radiant, and their faces shall never be ashamed." Psalm 34:5

Prayer: Lord, I have carried the burden of shame, but today I lay it at Your feet. Your Word declares that those who look to You will never be put to shame. I lift my eyes to You, Jesus, and I receive Your peace. Replace my shame with the radiance of Your love. I declare that I am no longer bound by my past, for You have set me free. Thank You for restoring my dignity and worth in You. In Jesus' name, Amen.

Prayer for Strength to Walk in Forgiveness Daily

Scripture: "Then Peter came to Jesus and asked, 'Lord, how many times shall I forgive my brother or sister who sins against me? Up to seven times?' Jesus answered, 'I tell you, not seven times, but seventy-seven times.'" Matthew 18:21-22

Prayer: Father, I confess that forgiveness is not always easy, but I choose to obey Your Word. Your Word tells us that we must forgive not just once, but seventy-seven times (Matthew 18:21-22). Teach me to forgive continually, as You have commanded, and to let go of any resentment or hurt that tries to take root in my heart. Help me not to keep a record of wrongs but to walk in the freedom of love, just as You have forgiven me. Strengthen me daily so that unforgiveness never finds a place in my heart and remind me that I am called to reflect Your grace in all circumstances. May my life be a testimony of Your endless mercy, and may my heart be filled with the peace that comes from walking in forgiveness. In Jesus' name, Amen.

Prayer for Complete Healing Through Forgiveness

Scripture: "He heals the brokenhearted and binds up their wounds." Psalm 147:3

Prayer: Lord, I know that true healing comes through forgiveness. Your Word says, "He heals the brokenhearted and binds up their wounds" (Psalm 147:3). I surrender every wound, every betrayal, and every painful memory to You. I trust that You see the depths of my pain and that Your healing touch is more powerful than any hurt I've experienced. Heal my heart, Lord, and bind up my wounds. I choose to release those who have hurt me, knowing that my healing is in Your hands, and that holding onto bitterness only hinders the peace You desire for me. Let Your love wash over me, bringing complete restoration and peace. Heal the broken places within me and make me whole again. I praise You for the healing work You are doing in my life, for the strength You provide to forgive, and for the freedom that comes with releasing the past. May Your peace guard my heart and mind as You continue to restore and renew me. In Jesus' name, Amen.

Prayers Regarding Healing

Prayer for Healing Through Jesus' Sacrifice

Scripture: "But He was wounded for our transgressions, He was bruised for our iniquities; the chastisement for our peace was upon Him, and by His stripes we are healed." Isaiah 53:5

Prayer: Father, I thank You for sending Jesus to bear my sins, sickness, and pain. Your Word in Isaiah 53:5 declares that by His stripes I am healed. I claim this promise over my life today. I rebuke every illness and declare that my body is restored because of the sacrifice of Jesus. I stand in faith, thanking You for my healing. In Jesus' name, Amen.

Prayer Against the Spirit of Infirmity

Scripture: "For God has not given us a spirit of fear, but of power and of love and of a sound mind." 2 Timothy 1:7

Prayer: Lord, I rebuke the spirit of infirmity that seeks to torment my body. According to 2 Timothy 1:7, I have not been given a spirit of fear but of power, love, and a sound mind. I declare healing, peace, and strength over my life. Sickness has no authority here, and I claim victory through Christ. Amen.

Prayer for Healing and Deliverance

Scripture: "The righteous cry out, and the Lord hears, and delivers them out of all their troubles." Psalm 34:17

Prayer: Heavenly Father, I cry out to You as my deliverer. Your Word promises in Psalm 34:17 that You hear the cries of the righteous and deliver them from all their troubles. I place my trust in Your faithfulness, knowing that You are near to the brokenhearted and that You are my refuge and strength in times of need. I ask You to deliver me from every sickness, pain, and affliction that weighs heavy on my body and spirit. I speak healing over every area of my life, and I declare freedom from all that hinders my health and well-being. May Your divine healing flow through me, bringing restoration and strength. Thank You, Lord, for Your love and care. I trust in Your ability to heal and restore, and I stand on the promise that by Your stripes, I am made whole. In Jesus' name, Amen.

Prayer to Uproot Sickness at Its Source

Scripture: "Every plant which My heavenly Father has not planted will be uprooted." Matthew 15:13

Prayer: Lord, I stand on Matthew 15:13 and declare that every sickness, disease, or affliction not planted by You is uprooted and destroyed in my life. I release Your healing power over my body, believing in Your perfect will to restore me. Thank You for breaking every chain of sickness. Amen.

Prayer for Strength During the Battle

Scripture: "But those who wait on the Lord shall renew their strength; they shall mount up with wings like eagles, they shall run and not be weary, they shall walk and not faint." Isaiah 40:31

Prayer: Father, I feel weak, but I hold on to Your promise in Isaiah 40:31 that as I wait on You, my strength will be renewed. I declare that I will not grow weary in this battle for my health. Empower me with the strength to overcome and let Your healing power flow through my body. In Jesus' name, Amen.

Prayer Declaring Victory Over Sickness

Scripture: "No weapon formed against you shall prosper." Isaiah 54:17

Prayer: Lord, I declare Your Word in Isaiah 54:17 that no weapon formed against me, including sickness, shall prosper. I command every illness to bow to the name of Jesus and proclaim victory over my health. I am healed and whole through the power of Your Word and Your Spirit. Amen.

Prayer for Healing of the Mind and Body

Scripture: "You will keep him in perfect peace, whose mind is stayed on You, because he trusts in You." Isaiah 26:3

Prayer: Lord, I ask for Your healing power to flow through every part of my body. Restore what is broken, renew what is weary, and strengthen what is weak. I declare that by the stripes of Jesus, I am healed, and I claim that healing now in faith. I rebuke every sickness, pain, and discomfort, and I release the full power of Your healing into my life.

Father, I also pray for emotional healing. Heal every wound, every hurt, and every painful memory that holds me captive. Bring restoration to relationships and peace to my spirit. Let

Your presence surround me, filling me with joy and strength to face each day with hope.

I trust in Your Word, which says that You are near to the brokenhearted and save those who are crushed in spirit (Psalm 34:18). I place my trust in You, knowing that You are my refuge and strength, a very present help in times of trouble (Psalm 46:1). Thank You for Your faithfulness, for Your peace, and for Your healing touch. In the mighty name of Jesus, I pray. Amen.

Prayer for Deliverance from Chronic Illness

Scripture: "For I will restore health to you and heal you of your wounds, says the Lord." Jeremiah 30:17

Prayer: Lord, I refuse to accept chronic illness as my portion. Your Word in Jeremiah 30:17 declares, "But I will restore you to health and heal your wounds," and I stand firm on this promise. I claim Your healing power over my life, knowing that You are the God who restores, renews, and makes all things new. I command all chronic conditions, ailments, and any affliction in my body to leave, in Jesus' name. I declare that my body is the temple of the Holy Spirit, and it is created to reflect Your perfect health and vitality. I ask for Your healing touch to flow through every area of my body—restoring, strengthening, and making me whole. I trust in Your faithfulness to heal and restore, and I believe that Your power is greater than any sickness or disease. Thank You for Your love, Your mercy, and Your promise of restoration. I rejoice in the healing that is already taking place and trust that I will see the full manifestation of Your power in my life. In Jesus' name, Amen.

Prayer for the Healing Power of the Holy Spirit

Scripture: "But if the Spirit of Him who raised Jesus from the dead dwells in you, He who raised Christ from the dead will also give life to your mortal bodies through His Spirit who dwells in you." Romans 8:11

Prayer: Holy Spirit, I invite You to breathe life into my mortal body. Romans 8:11 declares that the same Spirit who raised Jesus from the dead gives life to me. Let Your resurrection power flow through me, healing every area of my body—restoring strength, renewing my mind, and revitalizing my soul. I surrender every weakness, sickness, and burden to You, trusting in Your perfect power to make me whole. Fill me with Your peace and let Your presence dwell in me richly. Thank You for the life, vitality, and divine health You bring. I receive it by faith and give You all the glory. Amen.

Prayer for Complete Wholeness

Scripture: "Beloved, I pray that you may prosper in all things and be in health, just as your soul prospers." 3 John 1:2

Prayer: Father, I pray for complete wholeness—body, soul, and spirit. Your Word in 3 John 1:2 assures me that it is Your will for me to prosper and be in health as my soul prospers. I speak alignment over every part of my life, declaring Your perfect healing power. Let every broken place be restored, every weary heart be strengthened, and every anxious thought be replaced with Your peace. Renew my mind, purify my heart, and refresh my spirit so that I may walk in the fullness of Your promises. I receive Your divine health, abundant provision, and supernatural peace. Thank You, Lord, for making me whole and for completing the good work You have begun in me. I trust in Your unfailing love and stand on Your Word, knowing that in You, I lack nothing. In Jesus' name, Amen.

Prayer for Healing and Restoration

Scripture: "Heal me, O Lord, and I shall be healed; save me, and I shall be saved, for You are my praise." Jeremiah 17:14

Prayer: Lord, I come to You, declaring Jeremiah 17:14 over my life. Heal me, and I shall be healed. Restore what has been broken in my body and spirit. I praise You, knowing that Your power is greater than any illness or infirmity. Thank You for being my Healer and Savior. In Jesus' name, Amen.

Prayer to Break Generational Curses of Sickness

Scripture: "Christ has redeemed us from the curse of the law, having become a curse for us." Galatians 3:13

Prayer: Father, I stand on Galatians 3:13 and declare that through Christ, I am redeemed from every curse, including generational sickness. I break every chain of inherited illness in Jesus' name. I decree that Your blood covers me, bringing healing and freedom from every affliction passed down through my family line. Amen.

Prayer for Healing in the Name of Jesus

Scripture: "And whatever you ask in My name, that I will do, that the Father may be glorified in the Son." John 14:13

Prayer: Jesus, I call on Your name, knowing that John 14:13 promises that whatever I ask in Your name, You will do. I come before You today, asking for complete healing in my body, mind, and spirit. Lord, You are the Great Physician, the Healer of all things, and I believe in the power of Your name to restore me to wholeness. I ask that You bring healing to every area of my life—physical, emotional, and mental. Heal my body from sickness and pain, renew my mind from worry and fear, and restore my spirit with peace and joy. I trust that You know the depth of my need and that Your grace is more than sufficient to meet it. Let Your name be glorified through my restoration. May others witness Your healing power and be drawn to Your greatness. I trust in the authority of Your name, which holds the power to make all things new. Thank You for Your love, Your grace, and Your unfailing ability to heal and restore. I believe that as I call on Your name, I will see the fullness of Your healing manifest in my life. In Jesus' name, Amen.

Prayer for Renewed Health and Strength

Scripture: "He gives power to the weak, and to those who have no might He increases strength." Isaiah 40:29

Prayer: Lord, I feel weak, but I trust in Your promise from Isaiah 40:29. You give power to the weak and increase strength to the weary. Renew my strength and restore my health, Father. Let Your healing power flow through every part of my body. In Jesus' name, Amen.

Prayer Against Fear and Sickness

Scripture: "Do not fear, for I am with you; do not be dismayed, for I am your God. I will strengthen you and help you; I will uphold you with My righteous right hand." Isaiah 41:10

Prayer: Father, I reject fear, for You are with me. I claim Isaiah 41:10, knowing that You will strengthen me, help me, and uphold me with Your righteous hand. You are my refuge and my fortress, my God in whom I trust. I declare that sickness, fear, and anxiety have no place in my life, for I am covered by the blood of Jesus and filled with Your perfect peace. Let Your healing power flow through me, restoring every part of my body, mind, and spirit. I stand on Your promises, knowing that You are my ever-present help, my healer, and my sustainer. Thank You for Your unfailing love, Your faithfulness, and the victory I have in You. In Jesus' mighty name, Amen.

Prayer for Faith to Receive Healing

Scripture: "And the prayer of faith will save the sick, and the Lord will raise him up." James 5:15

Prayer: Lord, I come in faith, believing in Your promise in James 5:15 that the prayer of faith will save the sick. I trust You to raise me up and restore me completely. Strengthen my faith to receive Your healing power and stand on Your Word. Thank You, Father, for hearing my prayers. Amen.

Prayer to Rebuke the Enemy's Attack on My Health

Scripture: "Behold, I give you the authority to trample on serpents and scorpions, and over all the power of the enemy, and nothing shall by any means hurt you." Luke 10:19

Prayer: Lord, I take the authority You have given me in Luke 10:19, where You promised that I have the power to trample on serpents and scorpions, and to overcome all the power of the enemy. I stand firm in this authority today, rebuking every attack of sickness, disease, and infirmity in my life. I declare that no weapon formed against me will prosper, and that nothing will harm me because Your power is at work in me. I am covered by the blood of Jesus, and I stand in the victory You have already won on the cross. I claim healing and protection over my body, mind, and spirit, knowing that You are my shield and my deliverer. Thank You, Lord, for the victory I have in You. I trust in Your promises and believe that by Your power, every attack of the enemy is defeated. I walk in the fullness of Your healing and declare that Your strength is made perfect in my weakness. In Jesus' name, Amen.

Prayer for Healing Through God's Word

Scripture: "He sent His word and healed them, and delivered them from their destructions." Psalm 107:20

Prayer: Father, I thank You for sending Your Word to heal me, as You promised in Psalm 107:20. Let Your Word take root in my life, bringing healing and deliverance. I declare that Your Word is alive, powerful, and effective in restoring my health. In Jesus' name, Amen.

Prayer for Healing from Emotional Wounds

Scripture: "He heals the brokenhearted and binds up their wounds." Psalm 147:3

Prayer: Lord, I ask for healing not only for my body but also for my heart. Your Word in Psalm 147:3 promises that You heal the brokenhearted and bind up their wounds. Mend every emotional wound and bring peace to my soul. Thank You for Your tender love and care. Amen.

Prayer for Divine Health and Protection

Scripture: "Because you have made the Lord, who is my refuge, even the Most High, your dwelling place, no evil shall befall you, nor shall any plague come near your dwelling." Psalm 91:9-10

Prayer: Lord, I declare Psalm 91:9-10 over my life today. Because You are my refuge and my dwelling place, I stand firm on Your promise that no evil will befall me, and no plague will come near my home. I trust in Your protection and know that You are my fortress, my God, in whom I trust. I decree divine health and supernatural protection over myself, my family, and all those I love. May Your angels encamp around us, guarding us from every danger and keeping us safe from harm. I thank You for being my shield, my fortress, and my protector. Your faithfulness is my shield, and in You, I find peace and security. Thank You, Lord, for Your covering and for the assurance that no weapon formed against us will prosper. I rest in Your promises, knowing that You are always watching over me. In Jesus' name, Amen.

Prayer to Anoint Oil

Scripture: Is anyone among you sick? Let them call the elders of the church to pray over them and anoint them with oil in the name of the Lord. And the prayer offered in faith will make the sick person well; the Lord will raise them up." James 5:14-15

Heavenly Father, I come before You in faith, trusting in Your power and grace. I ask that You bless this oil and sanctify it for Your holy purposes. Just as You used oil in Scripture to anoint kings, priests, and prophets, I now dedicate this oil to You. Let it be a symbol of Your presence, Your power, and Your healing.

Lord, I pray that as this oil is applied, it would be a sign of Your anointing, bringing comfort, healing, and protection. May it be a reminder of the Holy Spirit's work in our lives and the authority we have through Jesus Christ. I ask that You fill this oil with Your divine power to bring peace, restoration, and deliverance from all that is not of You.

In the name of Jesus, I pray that this oil would be used to break chains, heal sickness, and bring restoration to every area of life where it is applied. May Your will be done, and may Your name be glorified in all things.

Prayers on Overcoming Fear

Prayer to Trust in God's Protection

Scripture: "The Lord is my light and my salvation; whom shall I fear? The Lord is the strength of my life; of whom shall I be afraid?" Psalm 27:1

Prayer: Lord, You are my light and my salvation; therefore, I will not fear. As Psalm 27:1 declares, "The Lord is my light and my salvation—whom shall I fear? The Lord is the stronghold of my life—of whom shall I be afraid?" You are the strength of my life, and I declare that no enemy, circumstance, or fear can overpower me. I trust in Your protection and stand firm, knowing that You are with me in every situation. No matter what comes against me, I rest in the assurance that You are my refuge, my fortress, and my deliverer. I choose to walk in confidence, knowing that Your presence goes before me, surrounding me with Your love and safety. Thank You, Lord, for being my light in the darkness and my strength in times of weakness. I place all my trust in You, and I will not be shaken. In Jesus' name, Amen.

Prayer to Reject the Spirit of Fear

Scripture: "For God has not given us a spirit of fear, but of power and of love and of a sound mind." 2 Timothy 1:7

Prayer: Father, I declare that fear does not come from You, for Your Word in 2 Timothy 1:7 says You have given me power, love, and a sound mind. I reject the spirit of fear and replace it with faith, courage, and trust in You. In Jesus' name, Amen.

Prayer for Peace Amidst Fear

Scripture: "Peace I leave with you; My peace I give to you. Let not your heart be troubled, neither let it be afraid." John 14:27

Prayer: Lord Jesus, I come before You with a heart full of gratitude, acknowledging the peace You freely offer to me. Your Word in John 14:27 reminds me that You have given me peace—not as the world gives, but a perfect, eternal peace that cannot be shaken. I receive this peace now, and I choose to rest in it, knowing that You are with me.

I renounce all worry, anxiety, and fear that try to invade my thoughts and steal my joy. I declare that my heart will not be troubled, for I trust in Your promises and in Your love for me. I refuse to let fear take hold of my mind or my circumstances. Instead, I choose to focus on You, the Prince of Peace, and allow Your calming presence to fill every part of my being.

Lord, I ask that You would guard my heart and mind in Christ Jesus, as You have promised in Your Word. Let Your peace surround me like a shield, protecting me from the worries and distractions of life. May Your peace lead me in every decision, and guide me through every challenge, bringing comfort to my soul.

Thank You for the assurance that Your peace is not temporary but everlasting. I trust that no matter what I face, You are always near, offering peace and rest. In Your mighty name, I pray. Amen.

Prayer Declaring God's Presence

Scripture: "Fear not, for I am with you; be not dismayed, for I am your God. I will strengthen you, yes, I will help you." Isaiah 41:10

Prayer: Father, I take comfort in Your promise from Isaiah 41:10 that You are with me. I will not fear because You are my God. Strengthen me, help me, and uphold me with Your righteous hand. When I feel weak, be my strength; when I feel lost, be my guide. Remind me that no storm is greater than Your power and no darkness can overshadow Your light. Fill my heart with Your peace that surpasses all understanding, and let my faith be steadfast in every season. I place my trust in You, knowing that I am never alone. You are my refuge, my protector, and my ever-present help in times of trouble. Thank You for surrounding me with Your unfailing love. In Jesus' name, amen.

Prayer Against Fear of the Unknown

Scripture: "For I know the thoughts that I think toward you, says the Lord, thoughts of peace and not of evil, to give you a future and a hope." Jeremiah 29:11

Prayer: Lord, I trust in Your plans for my life, as declared in Jeremiah 29:11. I refuse to fear the unknown because I know Your thoughts toward me are for peace and hope. I place my future in Your hands, knowing that You are faithful. Lord, I choose to be strong and courageous, as You commanded in Joshua 1:9. I will not be afraid or dismayed, for You are with me wherever I go. Strengthen my heart and help me stand firm against fear. In Jesus' name, Amen.

Prayer for Freedom from Anxiety

Scripture: "Be anxious for nothing, but in everything by prayer and supplication, with thanksgiving, let your requests be made known to God." Philippians 4:6

Prayer: Lord, I choose to be anxious for nothing, as Philippians 4:6 instructs. I bring my fears and concerns to You in prayer, with thanksgiving, trusting that You will provide peace and answer my prayers. Thank You for freeing me from anxiety. Amen.

Prayer for Faith Over Fear

Scripture: "When I am afraid, I put my trust in You." Psalm 56

Prayer: Lord, when fear tries to overwhelm me, I will put my trust in You, as Psalm 56:3 declares, "When I am afraid, I will trust in You." I choose faith over fear, knowing that You are my constant source of peace and strength. In moments of uncertainty, I rely on Your unwavering power to carry me through every challenge and hardship. Thank You for being my refuge and my shield, guarding my heart and mind with Your perfect peace. I trust in Your promises and hold onto the truth that You are with me, even in the midst of life's storms. No fear can stand against Your mighty presence. I give You all my worries, knowing that You are in control and that You will never leave me. Thank You, Lord, for being my rock and my salvation. In Jesus' name, Amen

Prayer for Boldness in Spiritual Battles

Scripture: "The wicked flee when no one pursues, but the righteous are bold as a lion." Proverbs 28:1

Prayer: Father, I declare that I am bold as a lion because of the righteousness I have in Christ. I refuse to flee in fear from spiritual battles, knowing You fight for me. Strengthen me with boldness to stand firm in Your truth. Amen.

Prayer to Rebuke the Enemy's Lies

Scripture: "Submit to God. Resist the devil and he will flee from you." James 4:7

Prayer: Lord, I submit myself to You and resist the devil, as James 4:7 commands: "Submit yourselves, then, to God. Resist the devil, and he will flee from you." I rebuke every lie of fear and declare that the enemy must flee from my life, for Your Word says that I am more than a conqueror through Christ. I stand firm in Your authority and reject all the lies that the enemy tries to sow into my mind and heart. Thank You, Lord, for giving me the power and authority to overcome fear through the victory that Jesus won on the cross. I trust in Your promises, knowing that no weapon formed against me will prosper. I walk in the peace and freedom that You have already provided. In Jesus' name, Amen.

Prayer for Restful Sleep

Scripture: "I will both lie down in peace, and sleep; for You alone, O Lord, make me dwell in safety." Psalm 4:8

Prayer: Lord, I declare Psalm 4:8 over my life. I will lie down in peace and sleep, knowing that You alone make me dwell in safety. I reject fear and anxiety that disrupt my rest and trust in Your protection. Amen.

Prayer for God's Perfect Love to Cast Out Fear

Scripture: "There is no fear in love, but perfect love casts out fear." 1 John 4:18

Prayer: Father, I thank You for Your perfect love that drives out all fear, as 1 John 4:18 declares, "There is no fear in love. But perfect love drives out fear." I thank You that Your love is greater than any fear or anxiety I may face. Fill me with Your love, Lord, and let it flow through every part of my being, removing any fear or doubt that tries to take root in my heart. I choose to stand firm in Your perfect love, knowing that Your love protects, strengthens, and empowers me to face every challenge with confidence. I embrace the freedom that comes from trusting in Your love, and I declare that fear has no place in my life. I am free and fearless because You are with me, and Your love is my anchor. In Jesus' name, Amen.

Prayer for Protection from Evil

Scripture: "Though I walk through the valley of the shadow of death, I will fear no evil; for You are with me." Psalm 23:4

Prayer: Lord, even when I walk through dark and challenging times, I will fear no evil, as Psalm 23:4 promises. Your rod and staff comfort me, and I am secure in Your presence. Thank You for guiding me through every valley. Amen.

Prayer for Deliverance from Fear

Scripture: "I sought the Lord, and He heard me, and delivered me from all my fears." Psalm 34:4

Prayer: Lord, I seek You today, trusting in Your promise from Psalm 34:4 that You will deliver me from all my fears. "I sought the Lord, and He answered me; He delivered me from all my fears." I bring all my fears before You, knowing that You are faithful to hear my prayer and to set me free from every fear that tries to control me. Whether it is fear of the future, fear of failure, or fear of the unknown, I release it all into Your capable hands. Thank You for being my deliverer, for never leaving me nor forsaking me, and for providing a way of escape from the stronghold of fear. I trust in Your protection, Your love, and Your ability to free me. Amen.

Prayer to Overcome Fear of Man

Scripture: "The fear of man brings a snare, but whoever trusts in the Lord shall be safe." Proverbs 29:25

Prayer: Lord, I reject the fear of man, for it is a snare. Instead, I place my trust in You, as Proverbs 29:25 says, knowing that You will keep me safe. Help me to live boldly, fearing only You. Amen.

Prayer to Be Rooted in God's Power

Scripture: "The Lord is on my side; I will not fear. What can man do to me?" Psalm 118:6

Prayer: Father, I declare that You are on my side, and I will not fear. Psalm 118:6 reminds me that no man or circumstance can prevail against me when You are for me. You are my refuge, my shield, and my ever-present help in trouble. No weapon formed against me shall prosper, and every tongue that rises against me in judgment, You will condemn. I stand in the confidence of Your unfailing love, knowing that You fight my battles and make a way where there seems to be none. Fill my heart with unshakable faith, and let Your peace rule over every anxious thought. Thank You for being my defender, my fortress, and my victory. In Jesus' name, Amen.

Prayer for Strength in Weakness

Scripture: "My grace is sufficient for you, for My strength is made perfect in weakness." 2 Corinthians 12:9

Prayer: Lord, I embrace Your promise in 2 Corinthians 12:9 that Your grace is sufficient for me. "But He said to me, 'My grace is sufficient for you, for my power is made perfect in weakness.'" When fear makes me feel weak and overwhelmed, I trust in Your strength, which is made perfect in my weakness. I acknowledge that I am not capable on my own, but with You, I can do all things. Thank You for sustaining me in moments of vulnerability and fear, for providing the grace I need to stand firm. I rest in the assurance that Your power is greater than any weakness I face. You are my source of strength and peace. In Jesus' name, Amen.

Prayer to Remember God's Power

Scripture: "The Lord your God, who goes before you, He will fight for you." Deuteronomy 1:30

Prayer: Lord, I will not fear because You go before me and fight for me, as Deuteronomy 1:30 declares. I trust in Your power to overcome every battle I face. Thank You for being my warrior and protector. Amen.

Prayer for Victory Over Fear

Scripture: "For the battle is not yours, but God's." 2 Chronicles 20:15

Prayer: Father, I surrender every fear to You, knowing that the battle is not mine but Yours, as 2 Chronicles 20:15 states. I trust in Your power to fight for me and bring victory over fear. When I feel weak, remind me that Your strength is made perfect in my weakness. Help me to stand firm in faith, knowing that You go before me, and no enemy can stand against Your mighty hand. Fill my heart with Your perfect peace, which casts out all fear, and let my mind be anchored in Your promises. I choose to rest in Your unfailing love, believing that You are working all things for my good. Thank You for Your faithfulness, for being my defender, and for leading me into victory. In Jesus' name, Amen.

Prayer to Walk in Freedom from Fear

Scripture: "You shall know the truth, and the truth shall make you free." John 8:32

Prayer: Lord, I declare that Your truth sets me free from fear, as promised in John 8:32. I walk in the freedom that comes from knowing You and Your Word. Fear has no hold on me because I am rooted in Your truth. Amen.

Prayer to Remember God's Power

Scripture: "The Lord your God, who goes before you, He will fight for you." Deuteronomy 1:30

Prayer: Lord God, I thank You for the promise in Deuteronomy 1:30 that You go before me and fight for me. You are my defender, my shield, and my strong tower. When fear rises, remind me that the battles I face are not mine alone. You are with me, guiding my every step and clearing the path ahead. Help me to surrender my worries and doubts to You, trusting in Your might and perfect will. Lord, strengthen my faith to stand firm, knowing that no enemy or situation can prevail against Your power. You are victorious, and in You, I find my confidence and peace. Thank You, Lord, for being my constant refuge. In Jesus' name, Amen.

Prayer for Victory Over Fear

Scripture: "For the battle is not yours, but God's." 2 Chronicles 20:15

Prayer: Father in heaven, I praise You for the assurance found in 2 Chronicles 20:15—that the battles I face do not belong to me, but to You. Fear often tries to paralyze me, but I stand on the truth that You are the ultimate warrior, fighting on my behalf. Lord, I release my fears, my struggles, and my anxieties to You, for You are mighty to save. Teach me to stand still and witness the salvation of the Lord in my life. When fear whispers lies, remind me that You are greater than anything I face. I declare that through Christ, I have victory over every fear, every doubt, and every attack of the enemy. I thank You for going before me and making the way. In Your power, I will not be shaken. In Jesus' name, Amen.

Prayer to Walk in Freedom from Fear

Scripture: "You shall know the truth, and the truth shall make you free." John 8:32

Prayer: Lord Jesus, I thank You for the freedom that comes through Your truth, as You promised in John 8:32. Your Word declares that perfect love casts out fear, and I know that Your love is perfect and unchanging. I ask that You fill my heart and mind with the truth of who You are and who I am in You. Fear has no authority over my life because I belong to You, and You have set me free. Help me to walk boldly in this freedom, rooted in Your promises and guided by Your Spirit. When fear tries to return, remind me of the power and victory I have through Your sacrifice. Thank You, Lord, for breaking every chain and enabling me to live in peace, courage, and faith. I commit my thoughts, emotions, and future into Your hands, trusting You completely. In Your powerful name, Amen.

Prayers on Restoration

Prayer for Restoration of Joy

Scripture: "Restore to me the joy of Your salvation and uphold me by Your generous Spirit." Psalm 51:12

Prayer: Lord, I ask for the restoration of joy in my heart, as David prayed in Psalm 51:12. Life's struggles have left me weary, but I believe Your salvation is my strength. Uplift me with Your generous Spirit and fill my heart with the joy that comes from knowing You. Thank You for the peace and joy You provide. Amen.

Prayer for Restoration of Health

Scripture: "For I will restore health to you and heal you of your wounds, says the Lord." Jeremiah 30:17

Prayer: Father, I stand on Your promise in Jeremiah 30:17 that You will restore my health and heal my wounds. Whether physical, emotional, or spiritual, I surrender every area of brokenness to You. I trust in Your healing power to bring complete restoration to my body, mind, and spirit. In Jesus' name, Amen.

Prayer for Restored Relationships

Scripture: "He will turn the hearts of the fathers to their children, and the hearts of the children to their fathers." Malachi 4:6

Prayer: Lord, I pray for the restoration of relationships in my life, as promised in Malachi 4:6, "He will turn the hearts of the parents to their children, and the hearts of the children to their parents." Turn hearts back to one another, heal divisions, and mend broken bonds. I ask for Your healing touch to restore love, trust, and understanding in my family, friendships, and all relationships that have been strained or wounded. Let Your love and peace reign in these connections, bringing reconciliation where there has been conflict and harmony where there has been discord. I trust in Your power to bring unity, and I believe that through You, all things can be made whole again. In Jesus' name, Amen.

Prayer for Financial Restoration

Scripture: "I will repay you for the years the locusts have eaten." Joel 2:25

Prayer: Lord, I claim the promise in Joel 2:25 that You will repay me for the years the locusts have eaten. Restore what was lost or stolen in my finances. I trust You as my provider and declare that lack and poverty have no place in my life. Thank You for bringing abundance and blessing. Amen.

Prayer for Spiritual Renewal

Scripture: "Create in me a clean heart, O God, and renew a steadfast spirit within me." Psalm 51:10

Prayer: Lord, I come to You with a humble heart, asking for spiritual renewal. As David prayed in Psalm 51:10, "Create in me a clean heart, O God, and renew a steadfast spirit within me," I seek Your cleansing touch and the restoration of a pure heart. Draw me closer to You, Lord, and renew my passion for prayer, worship, and Your Word. I confess any areas of my life where I have grown complacent or distant, and I ask for Your Holy Spirit to ignite a fresh fire within me. Fill me with a deep desire to seek You daily and to live according to Your will. Restore my joy in Your presence and renew my commitment to follow You wholeheartedly. In Jesus' name, Amen.

Prayer for Hope to Be Restored

Scripture: "Return to the stronghold, you prisoners of hope. Even today I declare that I will restore double to you." Zechariah 9:12

Prayer: Lord, restore hope to my heart as Zechariah 9:12 promises. Even when life feels overwhelming, I will hold on to You, my stronghold. I trust that You will restore double blessings for the trials I have endured. Thank You for being my source of hope. Amen.

Prayer for Restoration of Peace

Scripture: "And the peace of God, which surpasses all understanding, will guard your hearts and minds through Christ Jesus." Philippians 4:7

Prayer: Father, I ask for the restoration of peace in my life. Your Word in Philippians 4:7 promises that the peace of God, which surpasses all understanding, will guard my heart and mind in Christ Jesus. I pray that Your peace would settle over me, guarding me from anxiety, fear, and worry. Remove the turmoil that threatens my peace, and replace it with Your calm assurance. Help me to rest in the knowledge that You are in control, and that nothing can separate me from Your love. Fill me with Your peace that transcends circumstances and reminds me that You are my constant source of security.

Prayer for Restoring What the Enemy Stole

Scripture: "The thief does not come except to steal, and to kill, and to destroy. I have come that they may have life, and that they may have it more abundantly." John 10:10

Prayer: Lord Jesus, I thank You for the abundant life You have promised me in John 10:10. You came to give me life, and life to the fullest, and I declare that promise over my life today. I reject the plans of the enemy who seeks to steal, kill, and destroy, and I stand firm in the authority of Your Word.

I rebuke every lie, every attack, and every form of destruction that the enemy has brought into my life. I claim victory over every area where the enemy has tried to cause loss or harm, and I ask for Your restoration and healing. Restore to me everything that has been taken—my peace, my joy, my health, my relationships, and my purpose.

Lord, help me to walk in the fullness of Your blessings. Open my eyes to the abundant life You have already provided and give me the strength and wisdom to step into all that You have prepared for me. May I live in the overflow of Your goodness, and may Your blessings be a testimony to Your faithfulness.

Thank You, Jesus, for Your love, Your grace, and for the victory You have won on the cross. I trust in Your promises and rest in Your abundant life. In Your mighty name, I pray. Amen.

Prayer for Renewed Strength

Scripture: "But those who wait on the Lord shall renew their strength." Isaiah 40:31

Prayer: Lord, as Isaiah 40:31 says, "But those who hope in the Lord will renew their strength. They will soar on wings like eagles; they will run and not grow weary, they will walk and not be faint." I wait on You, trusting that You will renew my strength. When I feel weary and drained, I choose to place my hope in You. Restore my energy and my ability to move forward, even in the midst of fatigue. I declare that, through Your grace, I will rise up with wings like eagles, soaring above the challenges I face. I will run without growing weary and walk without fainting because You are my strength. Thank You for lifting me up and empowering me to keep going. In Jesus' name, Amen.

Prayer for Marital Restoration

Scripture: "What therefore God has joined together, let not man separate." Mark 10:9

Prayer: Father, I pray for the restoration of my marriage. According to Mark 10:9, what You have joined together, let no one separate. Heal broken communication, rebuild trust, and restore love. Let our union reflect Your grace and covenant. In Jesus' name, Amen.

Prayer for Restoration of Faith

Scripture: "Now faith is the substance of things hoped for, the evidence of things not seen." Hebrews 11:1

Prayer: Lord, I ask You to restore my faith, as Hebrews 11:1 declares, "Now faith is confidence in what we hope for and assurance about what we do not see." Strengthen my trust in Your promises, even when I cannot see the outcome or understand the journey. Help me to walk by faith, not by sight, and to trust that You are working all things for my good, even when I don't have all the answers. Renew my confidence in Your faithfulness and Your perfect timing. I choose to believe in Your goodness and to rest in the assurance that You are in control. In Jesus' name, Amen.

Prayer for a Restored Mind

Scripture: "Be transformed by the renewing of your mind." Romans 12:2

Prayer: Father, transform me by the renewing of my mind, as Romans 12:2 instructs. Restore my thoughts to align with Your Word and will. Break every stronghold of negativity and replace it with truth, hope, and peace. In Jesus' name, Amen

Prayer for Family Restoration

Scripture: "Believe on the Lord Jesus Christ, and you will be saved, you and your household." Acts 16:31

Prayer: Lord, I believe in Your promise in Acts 16:31 that salvation extends to my household. Restore broken relationships in my family and bring healing and unity. Let Your love and salvation flow through every member of my household. Amen.

Prayer for a Restored Spirit

Scripture: "The Lord is near to those who have a broken heart and saves such as have a contrite spirit." Psalm 34:18

Prayer: Lord, You are near to the brokenhearted, as Psalm 34:18 says. Restore my spirit, heal my wounds, and give me the strength to move forward. I surrender my pain to You and trust in Your loving care. Amen.

Prayer for Restoration of Confidence

Scripture: "Do not throw away your confidence, which has great reward." Hebrews 10:35

Prayer: Lord, restore my confidence, as Hebrews 10:35 reminds me of its great reward. Help me to trust in Your promises and to step forward boldly, knowing that You are with me. Strengthen my faith and courage. Amen.

Prayer for Restoration of Time

Scripture: "So teach us to number our days, that we may gain a heart of wisdom." Psalm 90:12

Prayer: Lord, I ask for the restoration of time lost to distractions, mistakes, and delays. As Psalm 90:12 says, "Teach us to number our days, that we may gain a heart of wisdom," I pray for wisdom in how I use my time. Help me to be mindful of the moments I have and to prioritize what truly matters. Teach me to redeem the time, to walk in Your perfect will, and to make the most of every opportunity You give me. Remove any hindrances that have kept me from walking fully in Your plans, and grant me the grace to move forward with purpose and clarity. May my time be used to glorify You and to fulfill the calling You have placed on my life. In Jesus' name, Amen.

Prayer for Restoration of Purpose

Scripture: "The plans of the Lord stand firm forever, the purposes of His heart through all generations." Psalm 33:11

Prayer: Father, restore my sense of purpose. I trust in Psalm 33:11 that Your plans and purposes for my life stand firm. Reveal Your will for me and guide me to walk in it fully. Renew my passion to fulfill the calling You have placed on my life. Amen.

Prayer for Revival in the Church

Scripture: "If My people who are called by My name humble themselves, pray, seek My face, and turn from their wicked ways, then I will hear from heaven, and will forgive their sin and heal their land." 2 Chronicles 7:14

Prayer: Lord, I come before You, asking for the restoration and revival of Your Church, as promised in 2 Chronicles 7:14: "If my people, who are called by my name, will humble themselves and pray and seek my face and turn from their wicked ways, then I will hear from heaven, and I will forgive their sin and will heal their land." Let us, Your people, humble ourselves before You, pray earnestly, seek Your face, and turn from any sin that hinders Your work in us. Bring healing to our communities and nations, Lord. Revive our hearts, renew our spirits, and stir up a hunger for You like never before. Let the fire of revival spread across the world, transforming lives, communities, and nations. May Your Church rise up with boldness, compassion, and conviction to spread the message of Your love and grace. In Jesus' name, Amen.

Prayer for Emotional Restoration

Scripture: "He heals the brokenhearted and binds up their wounds." Psalm 147

Prayer: Father, I bring my emotional wounds to You, trusting in Psalm 147:3 that You heal the brokenhearted. Restore my heart and bring peace to my emotions. Replace sorrow with joy and despair with hope. Thank You for being my healer. Amen.

Prayer for Restoration of God's Favor

Scripture: "For His anger is but for a moment, His favor is for life; weeping may endure for a night, but joy comes in the morning." Psalm 30:5

Prayer: Lord, I thank You that Your favor lasts a lifetime, as Psalm 30:5 declares. Restore Your favor in my life, and let joy replace every season of weeping. I trust in Your goodness and believe that brighter days are ahead. In Jesus' name, Amen.

Prayers Commanding Angels To Help You

Prayer for Angelic Protection

Scripture: "For He shall give His angels charge over you, to keep you in all your ways." Psalm 91:11

Prayer: Heavenly Father, I thank You for giving Your angels charge over me, as promised in Psalm 91:11. I command Your angels to surround me and protect me from every danger and attack of the enemy. Let them guard my steps and shield me from harm. In Jesus' name, Amen.

Prayer for Angelic Help in Spiritual Battles

Scripture: "The angel of the Lord encamps all around those who fear Him, and delivers them." Psalm 34:7

Prayer: Lord, I ask for Your angelic hosts to encamp around me, as You promised in Psalm 34:7. Deliver me from every spiritual attack and help me to stand firm against the schemes of the enemy. Thank You for Your divine protection. Father, thank You for sending angels before me, as You promised in Exodus 23:20. I command them to lead and guide me into the plans and purposes You have prepared for me. Let them make the way straight and protect me from harm. In Jesus' name, Amen.

Prayer for Angelic Assistance in Deliverance

Scripture: "And at that time your people shall be delivered, everyone who is found written in the book." Daniel 12:1

Prayer: Lord, I call upon Your angels to fight on my behalf, just as You sent Michael in Daniel 12:1, to protect and deliver Your people. I trust in Your divine protection, knowing that You send Your angels to surround me and guard me in all my ways. Deliver me from every stronghold of the enemy and rescue me from every snare and danger that seeks to harm me. I ask for Your angels to intervene on my behalf, to protect my family, my health, my mind, and my spirit from all forces of darkness. Thank You, Lord, for Your faithful and powerful help, for You are my refuge and my fortress. I stand firm in the assurance that Your protection is always with me. In Jesus' name, Amen.

Prayer for Angelic Help in Times of Fear

Scripture: "He will command His angels concerning you to guard you in all your ways." Psalm 91:11

Prayer: Father, when fear arises, I trust in Your Word from Psalm 91:11, which promises, "For He will command His angels concerning you to guard you in all your ways." I command Your angels to guard me and keep me in peace. Surround me with their presence, and let their strength drive away all fear. I declare that no fear, anxiety, or doubt will have a hold on me, for I am protected by Your mighty angels. Thank You, Lord, for Your divine protection and for filling me with peace that surpasses all understanding. In Jesus' name, Amen.

Prayer for Angels to Carry Out God's Will

Scripture: "Bless the Lord, you His angels, who excel in strength, who do His word, heeding the voice of His word." Psalm 103:20

Prayer: Lord, I declare Your Word over my life, knowing that Your angels heed the voice of Your Word, as Psalm 103:20 says, "Praise the Lord, you His angels, you mighty ones who do His bidding, who obey His Word." I release Your Word into the atmosphere, commanding Your angels to carry out Your will in my life. I ask that they bring about the answers to my prayers according to Your promises. Let Your angels be sent to work on my behalf, bringing provision, protection, healing, and breakthrough as You have spoken. I trust that as Your Word is declared, it will not return void but will accomplish all that You intend. Thank You for the power and authority You have given me in Christ. In Jesus' name, Amen.

Prayer for Angelic Intervention in Danger

Scripture: "But at night an angel of the Lord opened the prison doors and brought them out." Acts 5:19

Prayer: Father, just as Your angel delivered Peter from prison in Acts 5:19, I command angels to intervene in my life wherever danger or captivity exists. Open every closed door and deliver me from bondage. In Jesus' name, Amen.

Prayer for Angels to Fight Spiritual Battles

Scripture: "And war broke out in heaven: Michael and his angels fought with the dragon." Revelation 12:7

Prayer: Lord, I ask You to release Michael and Your heavenly armies to fight on my behalf, as they did in Revelation 12:7. I command Your angels to wage war against the forces of darkness trying to hinder my life. In Jesus' name, Amen.

Prayer for Angelic Help in Temptation

Scripture: "Then the devil left Him, and behold, angels came and ministered to Him." Matthew 4:11

Prayer: Lord, as Matthew 4:11 tells us that angels ministered to Jesus after His temptation, I ask for Your angels to minister to me in my times of weakness. When I face trials and temptations, I pray for Your divine strength and help to stand firm. Empower me to resist the lies of the enemy and to remain steadfast in Your Word. May Your angels surround me with comfort, encouragement, and guidance, helping me to stay strong and faithful in every challenge I encounter. Thank You, Lord, for Your heavenly assistance, and for the strength You provide to overcome. In Jesus' name, Amen.

Prayer for Angels to Guard My Family

Scripture: "The Lord has established His throne in heaven, and His kingdom rules overall." Psalm 103:19-20

Prayer: Father, I declare Psalm 103:19-20 over my family: "The Lord has established His throne in heaven, and His kingdom rules overall. Praise the Lord, you His angels, you mighty ones who do His bidding, who obey His word." I command Your angels to guard and protect my loved ones, keeping them safe from harm, and surrounding them with Your divine protection. Let no weapon formed against them prosper, and may Your peace reign over their lives. I trust that Your angels are encamped around them, guarding them from every danger. Thank You, Lord, for Your faithful protection over my family. In Jesus' name, Amen.

Prayer for Angelic Watchfulness

Scripture: "Are they not all ministering spirits sent forth to minister for those who will inherit salvation?" Hebrews 1:14

Prayer: Lord, I thank You for sending Your angels to minister to me, as stated in Hebrews 1:14. I command them to stand watch over my home, my workplace, and every area of my life. Let them guard me day and night. In Jesus' name, Amen.

Prayer for Angelic Help in Decisions

Scripture: "An angel of the Lord appeared to Joseph in a dream." Matthew 1:20

Prayer: Father, just as You sent an angel to guide Joseph in Matthew 1:20, I ask for angelic help and divine direction in making decisions. Lead me in the right path and reveal Your perfect will for my life. Remove any confusion, fear, or doubt, and fill me with Your wisdom and peace. Open my heart to hear Your voice clearly and grant me the courage to follow where You lead. Let every step I take be aligned with Your purpose and bring glory to Your name. In Jesus' name, Amen.

Prayer for Angels to Provide Strength

Scripture: "Then an angel appeared to Him from heaven, strengthening Him." Luke 22:43

Prayer: Lord, as You sent an angel to strengthen Jesus in Luke 22:43, I ask for angelic help to strengthen me in my times of weakness. When I face trials, challenges, or moments of struggle, I trust that You are with me, ready to provide the strength and encouragement I need. Send Your angels to empower me to endure, to lift me up, and to help me overcome every obstacle. I declare that through Your strength, I can do all things, and I place my trust in Your divine assistance. Thank You for Your loving care and for sending heavenly support in my times of need. In Jesus' name, Amen.

Prayer for Angelic Deliverance from Evil

Scripture: "He sent His angel and delivered His servants who trusted in Him." Daniel 3:28

Prayer: Lord, just as You sent Your angel to deliver Shadrach, Meshach, and Abednego in Daniel 3:28, I command angels to deliver me from every form of evil and danger. I trust in Your mighty power to protect me and my loved ones from harm. Guard me from the attacks of the enemy and surround me with Your heavenly protection. Let Your angels be a shield around me, delivering me from every snare and danger. Thank You, Lord, for Your faithfulness and for the angels You send to guard and deliver me.

Prayer for Angelic Encounters

Scripture: "Do not forget to entertain strangers, for by so doing some have unwittingly entertained angels." Hebrews 13:2

Prayer: Father, help me to be mindful of Your presence and open to divine encounters, as Hebrews 13:2 reminds me. I pray for angelic encounters that will strengthen my faith and reveal Your plans. In Jesus' name, Amen.

Prayer for Angels to Protect My Path

Scripture: "He shall keep your foot from being caught." Proverbs 3:26

Prayer: Lord, I ask Your angels to guide and protect my path, as Proverbs 3:26 declares, "For the Lord will be your confidence and will keep your foot from being caught." Guard me from the traps set by the enemy and lead me safely in Your ways. I trust that You are directing my steps and surrounding me with Your protection. Let Your angels go before me, clearing the way, and standing guard against any danger, seen or unseen. Thank You, Lord, for Your constant care and for the divine help You send to keep me safe. In Jesus' name, Amen.

Prayer for Angelic Help in Worship

Scripture: "I heard the voice of many angels around the throne." Revelation 5:11

Prayer: Lord, as angels worship around Your throne in Revelation 5:11, I ask for their help to join in pure and holy worship. Let their presence inspire me to worship You in spirit and truth. In Jesus' name, Amen.

Prayer for Angelic Help in Times of Battle

Scripture: "Then Elisha prayed, and the Lord opened the servant's eyes, and he saw the mountain full of horses and chariots of fire." 2 Kings 6:17

Prayer: Lord, just as You opened the eyes of Elisha's servant in 2 Kings 6:17, I pray for the host of heaven to surround me in my battles. Let me be confident in knowing Your angels are fighting for me. In Jesus' name, Amen.

Prayer for Angelic Help in Proclaiming the Gospel

Scripture: "An angel of the Lord spoke to Philip, saying, 'Arise and go." Acts 8:26

Prayer: Lord, I ask for angelic help as I share the Gospel. Just as You directed Philip in Acts 8:26, when You said, "Now an angel of the Lord said to Philip, 'Go south to the road—the desert road—that goes down from Jerusalem to Gaza,'" I pray that You would guide me to people who need to hear the good news of Jesus. Let Your angels direct my steps, opening doors for conversations and leading me to those whose hearts are ready to receive Your Word. Empower me with boldness, wisdom, and compassion to share Your love, knowing that You are always with me, guiding my words and actions. Thank You for Your heavenly assistance as I walk in obedience to Your calling. In Jesus' name, Amen.

Prayer for Angelic Presence in My Life

Scripture: "Surely the Lord is in this place, and I did not know it." Genesis 28:16

Prayer: Lord, I thank You for the unseen presence of angels in my life. Just as Jacob recognized Your presence in Genesis 28:16, when he said, "Surely the Lord is in this place, and I was not aware of it," I pray that You would open my eyes to be more aware of the angels You've sent to minister to me. Let me sense their presence and be comforted by the knowledge that I am never alone. May Your glory surround me through their presence, and may I be reminded of Your constant protection and care. Thank You, Lord, for Your angels and for the ways You minister to me through them. Amen.

Prayers Regarding Breaking Soul Ties

Prayer for Identification of Ungodly Soul Ties

Scripture: "Search me, O God, and know my heart; test me and know my anxious thoughts." Psalm 139:23

Prayer: Lord, I ask You to search my heart and reveal any ungodly soul ties that may be hindering my walk with You. As Psalm 139:23 declares, "Search me, God, and know my heart; test me and know my anxious thoughts," I invite You to examine every part of me. Expose any connection, bond, or relationship that is not aligned with Your will. Give me the courage to break free from anything that is holding me back from fully living for You. Help me to walk in purity, holiness, and freedom, fully surrendered to Your love and purpose. Thank You for Your guidance and grace. In Jesus' name, Amen.

Prayer for Forgiveness

Scripture: "Forgive us our debts, as we also have forgiven our debtors." Matthew 6:12

Prayer: Heavenly Father, I forgive anyone connected to ungodly soul ties in my life. As Matthew 6:12 teaches, I release them to You and ask for Your forgiveness for any way I have contributed to these ties. Cleanse me by Your grace. In Jesus' name, Amen.

Prayer for Cutting Ungodly Connections

Scripture: "Therefore, come out from among them and be separate, says the Lord." 2 Corinthians 6:17

Prayer: Lord, I declare the separation of my soul from any ungodly ties, as instructed in 2 Corinthians 6:17, which says, "Therefore, come out from them and be separate, says the Lord. Touch no unclean thing, and I will receive you." I renounce all connections, relationships, and influences that are not pleasing to You. I break every link to anything that has kept me bound and ask You to set me apart for Your glory. Cleanse my heart and soul, and help me to walk in purity and holiness, fully surrendered to Your will. Thank You for Your power to break every chain and for the freedom You give. In Jesus' name, Amen.

Prayer for Emotional Healing

Scripture: "He heals the brokenhearted and binds up their wounds." Psalm 147

Prayer: Father, I ask You to heal my heart from the pain caused by ungodly soul ties. As Psalm 147:3 promises, You heal the brokenhearted and bind up their wounds. I surrender my emotional wounds to You and ask for Your healing touch to restore every area that has been hurt. Let Your love fill every broken place, bringing peace and wholeness to my heart. Remove any lingering pain and replace it with Your comfort, love, and joy. Thank You for Your faithfulness to heal me and for restoring my emotional well-being. In Jesus' name, Amen.

Prayer for Biblical Cleansing

Scripture: "Create in me a clean heart, O God, and renew a steadfast spirit within me." Psalm 51:10

Prayer: Lord, I ask for spiritual cleansing from any impurity caused by soul ties. As Psalm 51:10 declares, "Create in me a clean heart, O God, and renew a steadfast spirit within me," I surrender my heart to You, asking for Your purification and renewal. Wash me with the precious blood of Jesus, cleansing me from all unrighteousness. Remove any emotional or spiritual residue from past connections and restore my heart to a place of purity and holiness. I trust in Your transformative power to make me whole and to renew my spirit to walk closely with You. In Jesus' name, Amen.

Prayer for Breaking Physical Ties

Scripture: "Flee from sexual immorality." 1 Corinthians 6:18

Prayer: Lord, I come before You in repentance, acknowledging any physical connections that have led to ungodly soul ties. As 1 Corinthians 6:18 commands, I choose to flee from immorality and ask You to break every unhealthy bond that has been formed in my life. Purify my heart, mind, and body, Lord, and help me to honor You in all that I do. I declare that my body is Your temple, and I surrender it completely to You. Cleanse me from any defilement and fill me with Your holiness, restoring me to Your perfect will. Thank You for Your grace and for setting me free. In Jesus' name, Amen.

Prayer for Breaking Agreements with Darkness

Scripture: "What fellowship has light with darkness?" 2 Corinthians 6:14

Prayer: Father, I renounce every agreement I have made with darkness through ungodly relationships, knowingly or unknowingly. I break every soul tie, emotional bond, and spiritual connection that has drawn me away from You. As 2 Corinthians 6:14 declares, I refuse to be yoked with anything that is not of Your light. Purify my heart and mind, Lord, and fill every empty place with Your presence. Let no darkness remain in me—shine Your truth into every corner of my life. Restore my identity in You and lead me into relationships that honor and glorify Your name. I declare complete freedom and victory through the blood of Jesus. In Jesus' name, Amen.

Prayer for Freedom

Scripture: "So if the Son sets you free, you will be free indeed." John 8:36

Prayer: Lord Jesus, You have set me free, and I claim that freedom over every soul tie in my life, as John 8:36 declares, "So if the Son sets you free, you will be free indeed." I declare that every chain of ungodly connection is broken, and I am no longer bound. Let me walk in the fullness of liberty that You have given me, free from all past ties and influences that hinder my walk with You. Thank You, Lord, for the freedom You provide and for empowering me to live according to Your will. In Jesus' name, Amen.

Prayer for Strength to Let Go

Scripture: "Forget the former things; do not dwell on the past." Isaiah 43:18

Prayer: Father, give me the strength to let go of any relationships or memories that keep ungodly soul ties alive. As Isaiah 43:18 teaches, "Forget the former things; do not dwell on the past," help me to release all ties that are not aligned with Your will. Grant me the courage to move forward in You, embracing the new things You have for my life. Heal my heart from past hurts and help me to step into the freedom and wholeness that comes from fully trusting in You. Thank You for making all things new in my life. In Jesus' name, Amen.

Prayer for Renewed Identity in Christ

Scripture: "If anyone is in Christ, he is a new creation." 2 Corinthians 5:17

Prayer: Lord, I declare that I am a new creation in Christ, as 2 Corinthians 5:17 states. The old has passed away, and I step fully into the new life You have given me. I sever all soul ties that attempt to bind me to my past—every emotional, spiritual, and mental connection that is not of You. Let every chain be broken in the name of Jesus. Renew my identity in You alone, Father, and fill my heart with the truth of who I am in Christ. I choose to walk in freedom, healing, and wholeness, fully surrendered to Your will. In Jesus' name, Amen.

Prayer for Protection Against Future Ties

Scripture: "Above all else, guard your heart, for everything you do flows from it." Proverbs 4:23

Prayer: Lord, protect my heart from forming future ungodly soul ties. As Proverbs 4:23 instructs, help me to guard my heart and keep it aligned with Your Word. Lead me in wisdom and discernment. In Jesus' name, Amen.

Prayer for Discernment

Scripture: "Test all things; hold fast what is good." 1 Thessalonians 5:21

Prayer: Lord, give me discernment to recognize unhealthy connections. As 1 Thessalonians 5:21 teaches, help me to test all things and hold on to what is good. Guide me to form relationships that honor You. Amen.

Prayer to Break Generational Soul Ties

Scripture: "He visited the iniquity of the fathers upon the children to the third and fourth generation." Exodus 34:7

Prayer: Lord, I break every generational soul tie passed down through my family line, as mentioned in Exodus 34:7, which speaks of the iniquity passed down to the third and fourth generations. I renounce these ungodly ties in the name of Jesus, and I declare freedom for myself and my future generations. I ask that You sever any negative influence or bondage from past generations, and replace it with Your healing, love, and grace. Let Your redemptive work flow through my family line, bringing healing, freedom, and transformation for all those who come after me. In Jesus' name, Amen.

Prayer for Healing from Betrayal

Scripture: "The Lord is near to the brokenhearted." Psalm 34:18

Prayer: Father, I bring before You any betrayal tied to ungodly soul ties. As Psalm 34:18 says, "The Lord is close to the brokenhearted and saves those who are crushed in spirit," I ask for Your healing touch to mend my heart. Remove any pain caused by betrayal, and restore my trust in You. Help me to forgive, release the hurt, and walk in the freedom You provide. Strengthen my heart and draw me closer to You, knowing You are near in every moment of brokenness. In Jesus' name, Amen

Prayer for Breaking Emotional Ties

Scripture: "Cast all your anxiety on Him because He cares for you." 1 Peter 5:7

Prayer: Lord, I cast every emotional burden from ungodly soul ties upon You, as 1 Peter 5:7 instructs. Break these emotional chains and replace them with Your peace. In Jesus' name, Amen.

Prayer for Purity

Scripture: "Blessed are the pure in heart, for they shall see God." Matthew 5:8

Prayer: Lord, purify my heart from any defilement caused by ungodly soul ties. Break every connection that hinders my relationship with You, and sever every bond that does not align with Your will. Wash me clean with the power of Your Word and the blood of Jesus. As Matthew 5:8 declares, let my heart be pure so that I may see You clearly and walk in the fullness of Your presence. Fill every empty place with Your love, peace, and righteousness. In Jesus' name, Amen.

Prayer for Restoration of Relationships

Scripture: "If it is possible, as much as depends on you, live peaceably with all men." Romans 12:18

Prayer: Father, I pray for restoration in relationships that are in Your will and for the breaking of those that are not. As Romans 12:18 encourages, help me to live in peace with others while honoring You. Amen.

Prayer to Renounce Ungodly Ties

Scripture: "Submit to God. Resist the devil, and he will flee from you." James 4:7

Prayer: Lord, I submit to You and resist the devil's hold over any ungodly soul ties in my life, as James 4:7 commands, "Submit yourselves, then, to God. Resist the devil, and he will flee from you." I renounce these ties and declare that they have no power over me. I break every stronghold, and I choose to walk in the freedom and authority You've given me through Christ. Thank You for Your victory and for setting me free from any bondages that do not align with Your will. In Jesus' name, Amen.

Prayer for Godly Relationships

Scripture: "Iron sharpens iron, and one man sharpens another." Proverbs 27:17

Prayer: Father, bring godly relationships into my life that sharpen and encourage me, as Proverbs 27:17 teaches, "As iron sharpens iron, so one person sharpens another." Help me to form connections that glorify You and strengthen my faith. Lead me to people who will walk alongside me in truth, prayer, and encouragement, and who will help me grow in my relationship with You. I trust that You will surround me with those who will build me up in You, and I am open to the bonds You desire to form in my life. In Jesus' name, Amen.

Prayer for Complete Freedom

Scripture: "Where the Spirit of the Lord is, there is freedom." 2 Corinthians 3:17

Prayer: Lord, I thank You for the freedom found in Your Spirit, as 2 Corinthians 3:17 declares, "Now the Lord is the Spirit, and where the Spirit of the Lord is, there is freedom." I ask You to break every remaining soul tie that binds me and set me free from any unhealthy or ungodly connections. Fill me with the freedom and joy of Your presence and help me to walk in the liberty You have given me. Let Your Holy Spirit guide me, heal me, and empower me to live in the fullness of Your grace. In Jesus' name, Amen.

Prayers for Vindication

Prayer for God's Justice

Scripture: "The Lord is a God of justice; blessed are all who wait for Him!" Isaiah 30:18

Prayer: Lord, You are a God of justice. I come before You, trusting in Your timing and righteousness. As Isaiah 30:18 says, I wait on You to bring vindication in this situation. You see all things, and nothing is hidden from Your sight. Arise, O Lord, and be my defender. Let truth prevail and let every scheme of the enemy be exposed and defeated. Strengthen my heart as I wait on You and fill me with Your peace. I trust that You are working all things for my good and that Your justice will be done in Your perfect way. Show Your power and defend my cause, that Your name may be glorified. In Jesus' name, Amen.

Prayer for Deliverance from False Accusations

Scripture: "No weapon formed against you shall prosper, and every tongue which rises against you in judgment you shall condemn." Isaiah 54:17

Prayer: Father, I declare Isaiah 54:17 over my life: "No weapon formed against you shall prosper, and every tongue which rises against you in judgment, you shall condemn." I trust in Your protection and vindication. Every false accusation and slanderous tongue raised against me will be silenced by Your power. Lord, let no weapon of the enemy succeed, and surround me with Your favor and justice. I stand firm in Your promises, knowing that You are my Defender and Advocate.

Prayer for Vindication of Integrity

Scripture: "Vindicate me, O Lord, for I have walked in my integrity." Psalm 26:1

Prayer: Lord, I come to You with a heart that strives for integrity. As Psalm 26:1 declares, "Vindicate me, O Lord, for I have walked in my integrity. I have trusted also in the Lord; I shall not slip." I ask You to examine my heart and mind, revealing any areas that need Your purification. I trust that You will prove me innocent before my accusers and shield me with Your truth. Let my life reflect Your righteousness, and may Your justice prevail in all situations. In Jesus' name, Amen.

Prayer for God's Righteous Judgment

Scripture: "The Lord executes righteousness and justice for all who are oppressed." Psalm 103:6

Prayer: Lord, I am oppressed by unjust actions, but I trust in Your Word from Psalm 103:6. Execute Your righteousness and justice in my life. Fight on my behalf, and let truth prevail. In Jesus' name, Amen.

Prayer for God to Defend My Cause

Scripture: "Contend, Lord, with those who contend with me; fight against those who fight against me." Psalm 35:1

Prayer: Heavenly Father, I come before You, asking You to contend with those who contend with me, as Psalm 35:1 says, "Contend, O Lord, with those who contend with me; fight against those who fight against me." Fight on my behalf and bring justice to my cause. Stand strong against the schemes of the enemy and protect me from all harm. I trust in Your power and in Your ability to bring justice and victory. Let Your might be displayed, and may Your righteousness be my defense. In Jesus' name, Amen.

Prayer for Truth to Be Revealed

Scripture: "For nothing is hidden that will not be made manifest." Luke 8:17

Prayer: Lord, let the truth come to light as Luke 8:17 declares. Expose lies and deceit, and bring clarity to this situation. I trust You to reveal the truth and vindicate me. In Jesus' name, Amen.

Prayer for Strength While Waiting

Scripture: "Wait for the Lord; be strong and let your heart take courage." Psalm 27:14

Prayer: Father, as I wait for Your vindication, I ask You to strengthen my heart. Psalm 27:14 reminds me to "Wait on the Lord; be of good courage, and He shall strengthen your heart." Help me to take courage and trust in Your perfect timing, knowing that You are working on my behalf. Sustain me with Your grace and power, and give me peace as I wait on You. May I find comfort in Your promises, and may my faith be strengthened as I trust in Your faithfulness. In Jesus' name, Amen.

Prayer Against Injustice

Scripture: "Do not take revenge, my dear friends, but leave room for God's wrath." Romans 12:19

Prayer: Lord, I resist the urge to seek vengeance and instead place this injustice in Your hands, as Romans 12:19 instructs: "Do not avenge yourselves, but rather give place to wrath; for it is written, 'Vengeance is Mine, I will repay,' says the Lord." I trust in Your perfect justice and surrender this situation to You. Take control, and bring Your divine justice to this matter. Let Your will be done, and may Your peace fill my heart as I trust in Your ability to right all wrongs. In Jesus' name, Amen.

Prayer for Deliverance from Oppression

Scripture: "He will bring forth your righteousness as the light, and your justice as the noonday." Psalm 37:6

Prayer: Father, I trust in Your promise from Psalm 37:6, which says, "He shall bring forth your righteousness as the light, and your justice as the noonday." I ask You to bring my righteousness to light and my justice to be seen like the noonday sun. Deliver me from the oppression of the wicked, and let Your truth prevail in every situation. I trust that You will defend me and bring victory in Your perfect timing. Let Your justice shine through, and may Your peace reign in my heart. In Jesus' name, Amen.

Prayer for Restored Reputation

Scripture: "He will make your vindication shine like the dawn." Psalm 37:6

Prayer: Lord, I come before You asking for the restoration of my reputation. As Psalm 37:6 assures, "He shall bring forth your righteousness as the light, and your justice as the noonday." Let my vindication shine brightly, and let the truth be revealed in every circumstance. Clear my name and restore what has been unjustly taken. I trust in Your timing and Your perfect justice. May Your glory be seen as You work on my behalf. In Jesus' name, Amen.

Prayer for God's Defense

Scripture: "The Lord will fight for you; you need only to be still." Exodus 14:14

Prayer: Lord, I rest in the promise of Exodus 14:14. I know You will fight for me, and I choose to be still and trust in Your power. Vindicate me, O Lord, and bring glory to Your name. Amen.

Prayer for Protection Against Lies

Scripture: "Keep me safe, my God, for in You I take refuge." Psalm 16:1

Prayer: Lord, protect me from the lies and schemes of the enemy. As Psalm 16:1 says, I take refuge in You. Defend me against those who seek to harm me unjustly. In Jesus' name, Amen.

Prayer for Favor in Court or Legal Battles

Scripture: "For the Lord your God is He who goes with you, to fight for you against your enemies." Deuteronomy 20:4

Prayer: Father, as I stand in the midst of this legal battle, I place my full trust in Your Word and in Your ability to fight on my behalf. Deuteronomy 20:4 assures me that You go before me and fight for me against those who oppose me unjustly. I hold onto this promise with faith, knowing that You are my ultimate Advocate and Defender.

Lord, I ask that You go ahead of me in this situation. Clear the path before me and prepare the hearts and minds of those involved. Let Your justice prevail and let Your favor rest upon me. Surround me with wisdom, discernment, and peace throughout this process.

Father, I pray for Your protection over my reputation, my resources, and my peace of mind. Let Your will be done in this case, and may Your righteousness shine through. I trust that You will handle every detail with perfect wisdom and bring about a resolution that brings glory to Your name.

Thank You, Lord, for fighting for me. I surrender this battle into Your capable hands, and I trust that You will bring victory according to Your perfect will. In Jesus' name, I pray. Amen.

Prayer for Justice for the Oppressed

Scripture: "He has sent me to proclaim liberty to the captives." Luke 4:18

Prayer: Lord, I proclaim liberty over my life from every false accusation and oppression, as declared in Luke 4:18. You are my Deliverer and my Advocate, and I trust in Your justice. Set me free from the chains of injustice, fear, and burden, and restore my peace and joy. Let every lie be silenced and every scheme against me be overturned by Your mighty hand. Vindicate me in Your power, and let Your truth and righteousness prevail. I stand in the freedom You have given me, knowing that whom the Son sets free is free indeed. In Jesus' name, Amen.

Prayer for Confidence in God's Judgment

Scripture: "Shall not the Judge of all the earth do what is just?" Genesis 18:25

Prayer: Lord, I trust You as the righteous Judge. You see all things, and nothing is hidden from Your sight. As Genesis 18:25 declares, You will do what is just. I surrender my situation into Your hands, knowing that Your justice will prevail in Your perfect timing. Bring truth to light, defend me against every falsehood, and let righteousness be established. Strengthen my heart to wait on You with faith, knowing that You are always faithful. May Your will be done, and may Your name be glorified. In Jesus' name, Amen.

Prayer for Peace Amidst Accusations

Scripture: "The peace of God, which surpasses all understanding, will guard your hearts." Philippians 4:7

Prayer: Father, guard my heart with Your perfect peace, as Philippians 4:7 promises. Let Your peace, which surpasses all understanding, cover my mind and soul, keeping me steadfast in faith. Even amidst accusations and trials, I trust in Your vindication and justice. Strengthen me to stand firm, free from fear and anxiety, knowing that You are my Defender. Fill me with Your love, that I may respond with grace and wisdom. I rest in Your unfailing faithfulness, believing that You are working all things for my good. In Jesus' name, Amen.

Prayer for God to Silence My Enemies

Scripture: "The Lord will silence all flattering lips and every boastful tongue." Psalm 12

Prayer: Lord, silence the tongues of those who speak against me unjustly, as Psalm 12:3 declares. Let their words hold no power, and let truth prevail. In Jesus' name, Amen.

Prayer for Restoration of Honor

Scripture: "Instead of your shame, there shall be a double portion." Isaiah 61:7

Prayer: Lord, where shame has been brought upon me, I declare Isaiah 61:7. Restore my honor and give me a double portion of Your blessings. Vindicate me before all. In Jesus' name, Amen.

Prayer for Strength to Trust God's Justic

Scripture: "Trust in the Lord with all your heart and lean not on your own understanding." Proverbs 3:5

Prayer: Lord, I come before You with a heart full of trust, as Proverbs 3:5 instructs—trusting in You with all my heart and not relying on my own understanding. I acknowledge that Your ways are higher than my ways and Your thoughts higher than my thoughts. When I face challenges, I choose to lean on Your wisdom, Your guidance, and Your perfect justice, knowing that You are always in control.

I place this battle in Your hands, Lord. You are my Defender, my Stronghold, and my Help in times of trouble. I trust that You are fighting for me and that You will work all things together for my good, according to Your will. I release my worries and fears into Your hands and surrender my need to control the outcome.

Father, give me the strength to remain patient and the faith to trust in Your timing. I ask for Your peace to fill my heart as I wait on You, knowing that You will lead me through every difficulty and bring me to victory. Thank You for being faithful, for being my refuge, and for always being with me. I rest in Your promises, knowing You are with me in every battle. In Jesus' name, I pray. Amen.

Prayer for God's Vindication to Glorify His Name

Scripture: "Not to us, Lord, not to us, but to Your name be the glory." Psalm 115:1

Prayer: Father, as You bring vindication, I give all glory to Your name, as Psalm 115:1 declares. Let Your justice shine forth so others may see Your righteousness and be drawn to You. In Jesus' name, Amen.

Prayers Before Bed

Prayer for Divine Protection

Scripture: "The Lord will watch over your coming and going both now and forevermore." Psalm 121:8

Prayer: Heavenly Father, as I lay down to sleep, I trust in Your divine protection. Your Word in Psalm 121:8 assures me that You watch over me at all times. Shield me from any spiritual attacks or disturbances tonight. I commit myself to You and rest in the assurance of Your care. In Jesus' name, Amen.

Prayer to Guard My Mind

Scripture: "You will keep in perfect peace those whose minds are steadfast because they trust in You." Isaiah 26

Prayer: Father, I surrender my thoughts to You tonight. Isaiah 26:3 promises that You will keep me in perfect peace as my mind stays on You. I rebuke any intrusive or tormenting thoughts and declare peace over my mind as I sleep. In Jesus' name, Amen.

Prayer to Cancel Nightmares

Scripture: "God has not given us a spirit of fear, but of power and of love and of a sound mind." 2 Timothy 1:7

Prayer: Lord, I come against every spirit of fear, nightmare, or oppression that seeks to disturb my sleep. According to 2 Timothy 1:7, You have given me a spirit of power, love, and a sound mind. I cover my dreams with the blood of Jesus and declare peace over my sleep. Amen.

Prayer to Declare God's Presence

Scripture: "The angel of the Lord encamps around those who fear Him, and He delivers them." Psalm 34:7

Prayer: Lord, I thank You for Your constant love and faithfulness. I ask that You fill this room with Your presence, making it a sanctuary of peace and comfort. May Your Holy Spirit bring calm to my heart and mind, dispelling all fear and anxiety. Protect me from all evil and strengthen my spirit with Your grace. Let Your light shine brightly in the darkness and guide my steps as I rest in Your arms. May Your peace, which surpasses all understanding, guard my heart and mind tonight. In Jesus' name, Amen.

Prayer for Restful Sleep

Scripture: "In peace I will lie down and sleep, for You alone, Lord, make me dwell in safety." Psalm 4:8

Prayer: Father, I thank You for Your peace that surpasses all understanding. As I lie down tonight, I claim the promise of Psalm 4:8. I will sleep peacefully, knowing that You alone make me dwell in safety. In Jesus' name, Amen.

Prayer to Cover My Bedroom

Scripture: "No harm will overtake you, no disaster will come near your tent." Psalm 91:10

Prayer: Lord, I plead the blood of Jesus over my household tonight. According to Psalm 91:10, no harm or disaster will come near my home. Cover every corner of my house with Your presence, and let Your peace reign here. In Jesus' name, Amen.

Prayer Against Spiritual Attacks

Scripture: "Submit yourselves, then, to God. Resist the devil, and he will flee from you." James 4:7

Prayer: Father, I submit myself to You tonight and resist every plan of the enemy. Your Word in James 4:7 promises that when I resist the devil, he must flee. I cancel every spiritual attack aimed at me during the night and declare victory through Christ. Amen.

Prayer to Plead the Blood of Jesus

Scripture: "They triumphed over him by the blood of the Lamb and by the word of their testimony." Revelation 12:11

Prayer: Lord, I plead the blood of Jesus over my spirit, soul, and body. Revelation 12:11 declares that we triumph over the enemy by the blood of the Lamb. Let the blood of Jesus be a barrier against any evil that seeks to come near me tonight. Amen.

Prayer for Angelic Assistance

Scripture: "For He will command His angels concerning you to guard you in all your ways." Psalm 91:11

Prayer: Father, I also thank You for the power of Your Word, which promises that You are our refuge and fortress. I ask that You send Your angels to watch over every corner of this home, keeping it secure from any harm or danger. Surround my loved ones with Your divine protection, and may Your peace rest upon this household. Let Your angels minister comfort to me as I rest, and may I wake up refreshed and renewed in Your presence. In Jesus' name, Amen.

Prayer to Rebuke the Enemy

Scripture: "The Lord will cause your enemies who rise against you to be defeated before you." Deuteronomy 28:7

Prayer: Lord, I rebuke every plan of the enemy against me tonight. Deuteronomy 28:7 promises that You will cause my enemies to be defeated before me. Let no spiritual attack prevail, and let Your victory be manifest in my life. Amen.

Prayer to Renew Strength

Scripture: "He gives strength to the weary and increases the power of the weak." Isaiah 40:29

Prayer: Lord, I ask for renewed strength as I sleep tonight. Your Word in Isaiah 40:29 declares that You give strength to the weary. Refresh my body, mind, and spirit, and let me wake up ready to face a new day. In Jesus' name, Amen.

Prayer to Silence the Enemy's Voice

Scripture: "No weapon formed against you shall prosper, and you will refute every tongue that accuses you." Isaiah 54:17

Prayer: Father, I silence every voice of accusation, fear, or discouragement from the enemy. Isaiah 54:17 promises that no weapon formed against me shall prosper, and every tongue that rises against me in judgment, You will condemn. I declare this truth over my life tonight. Let Your peace guard my heart and mind, and let Your truth drown out every lie of the enemy. I take refuge in Your presence, knowing that You are my protector and my shield. No scheme of darkness can prevail against the light of Your love. I stand in victory, covered by Your grace and strengthened by Your Word. Thank You, Father, for being my defender and my refuge. In Jesus' name, Amen.

Prayer to Break Strongholds in Dreams

Scripture: "For the weapons of our warfare are not carnal but mighty in God for pulling down strongholds." 2 Corinthians 10:4

Prayer: Lord, I come against every demonic stronghold that may seek to infiltrate my dreams. 2 Corinthians 10:4 declares that the weapons of my warfare are mighty in You. I break every stronghold of fear, confusion, or torment in Jesus' name. I declare that my mind is covered by the blood of Jesus, and no weapon formed against me shall prosper. Let Your angels encamp around me as I sleep, and fill my spirit with Your peace. I rebuke every spirit of oppression and declare that only Your voice and truth will have access to my thoughts. Let my dreams be filled with Your presence, revelation, and divine rest. Thank You, Lord, for being my protector and for granting me perfect peace. In Jesus' mighty name, Amen.

Prayer to Declare God's Peace

Scripture: "And the peace of God, which transcends all understanding, will guard your hearts and your minds in Christ Jesus." Philippians 4:7

Prayer: Father, I come before You tonight with a heart full of gratitude. I release every worry, every care, and every burden into Your hands, trusting that You are more than able to carry them. Your Word in 1 Peter 5:7 encourages me to "cast all my anxiety on You, because You care for me," and tonight I surrender everything that weighs heavy on my heart. I trust You to handle every concern, knowing that You are my Provider, my Protector, and my ever-present help in times of need.

I thank You for Your promise in Philippians 4:7 that Your peace, which transcends all understanding, will guard my heart and mind in Christ Jesus. I ask for that peace to fill every corner of my being, bringing calm to my thoughts and rest to my soul. May Your peace surround me like a fortress, protecting my mind from any anxious thoughts or worries that may arise during the night.

As I lay down to sleep, I entrust all my concerns to You, knowing that You are at work even while I rest. I release control into Your hands, trusting that You are taking care of everything I cannot control. I know that Your plans for me are good, and I place my complete trust in Your perfect timing and provision.

Father, I thank You for Your faithfulness and Your constant presence in my life. I ask for Your angels to surround me, providing protection, rest, and safety throughout the night.

Let Your comfort and rest fill my heart, and let my sleep be peaceful, knowing that You are watching over me.

Thank You, Lord, for Your care, Your love, and Your protection. I trust in You completely tonight and always. May I awaken refreshed and renewed, ready to face a new day in Your grace. In Jesus' name, Amen.

Prayer to Confess God's Faithfulness

Scripture: "The steadfast love of the Lord never ceases; His mercies never come to an end; they are new every morning." Lamentations 3:22-23

Prayer: Lord, I thank You for Your steadfast love and faithfulness. Lamentations 3:22-23 reminds me that Your mercies are new every morning. I rest tonight in the assurance of Your love and care. Amen.

Prayer for the Power of the Cross

Scripture: "Having disarmed the powers and authorities, He made a public spectacle of them, triumphing over them by the cross." Colossians 2:15

Prayer: Lord Jesus, I thank You for the victory You secured for me through the cross. According to Colossians 2:15, You disarmed every power and authority of the enemy, making a public spectacle of them and triumphing over them. Tonight, I rest in that victory. I decree that no weapon formed against me in the spiritual realm can prosper because of the finished work of the cross. I break every assignment of the enemy sent to disturb my rest, hinder my peace, or infiltrate my dreams. I cover myself, my family, and my home with the power of the blood of Jesus. Let the victory of the cross be evident in my life as I rest in Your peace and presence. I declare that my sleep is blessed, and my soul is renewed because of the triumph You achieved for me. In Jesus' mighty name, Amen.

Prayer to Speak Blessings Over My Night

Scripture: "The Lord bless you and keep you; the Lord make His face shine on you and be gracious to you; the Lord turn His face toward you and give you peace." Numbers 6:24-26

Prayer: Heavenly Father, I stand on Your Word in Numbers 6:24-26 and declare Your blessings over my life, my family, and my home tonight. Lord, bless me and keep me under the shadow of Your wings. Let Your face shine upon me and be gracious to me as I rest. I ask for Your peace to fill every corner of my heart and mind, guarding me against any disturbance or spiritual attack. May Your presence surround my household, driving out all darkness and fear. I speak blessings over my dreams, declaring that they will be filled with visions of Your glory and purpose. Lord, may this night bring restoration, renewal, and divine alignment with Your will for my life. I surrender everything to You and trust in Your faithful protection. In the name of Jesus, I pray, Amen.

Prayer Against Night Oppression and Fear

Scripture: "You will not fear the terror of night, nor the arrow that flies by day." Psalm 91:5

Prayer: Lord Almighty, I come before You tonight, standing on the promise of Psalm 91:5. I declare that I will not fear the terror of the night or any attack of the enemy that seeks to harm me while I sleep. I know that You are my refuge and fortress, my God in whom I trust. Father, I ask You to send Your angels to stand guard around me and my home. Every spirit of fear, oppression, or torment that comes in the night is rebuked and cast out in the name of Jesus. I decree that the enemy has no authority over my life or my rest because I am covered by the blood of Jesus. Fill me with Your perfect peace and remind me that You have not given me a spirit of fear, but of power, love, and a sound mind. Thank You for being my shield and my defender. In Jesus' name, Amen.

Prayer for God's Light to Surround Me

Scripture: "The light shines in the darkness, and the darkness has not overcome it." John 1:5

Prayer: Father, I thank You that Your light shines in the darkness, and no power of the enemy can overcome it, as stated in John 1:5. Tonight, I ask for Your light to fill every area of my life, my home, and my spirit. Let Your presence drive out all darkness, fear, and oppression that may seek to enter my mind or dreams. Surround me with Your radiant light, Lord, and let it serve as a shield against any spiritual attacks. I declare that I walk in the light of Christ and that no evil has dominion over me. Lord, may Your light illuminate my path, even as I rest, guiding me into divine peace and safety. I trust in You completely to protect me through the night and wake me with the assurance of Your love and mercy. In Jesus' name, Amen.

Prayer for Gratitude, Trust, and Renewal

Scripture: "Give thanks in all circumstances; for this is God's will for you in Christ Jesus." 1 Thessalonians 5:18

Prayer: Lord, I come before You tonight with a heart full of gratitude. Your Word in 1 Thessalonians 5:18 reminds me to give thanks in all circumstances, for this is Your will for me in Christ Jesus. I thank You for the gift of life, for sustaining me throughout the day, and for the peace I have in You. As I lay down to sleep, I trust You with every area of my life—my past, my present, and my future. Lord, I release all my worries, fears, and anxieties into Your hands, knowing that You care for me.

Father, I ask for a divine renewal of my body, mind, and spirit tonight. Let Your Holy Spirit refresh me as I sleep, filling me with strength for the new day ahead. Surround me with Your love and protection, and let Your presence be tangible as I rest. I declare that no weapon formed against me shall prosper and that I will rise tomorrow full of joy, peace, and purpose. Thank You, Lord, for being my refuge and strength, my ever-present help in trouble. In Jesus' precious name, I pray, Amen.

Prayers to Cancel Bad Dreams

Prayer for Protection in Sleep

Scripture: "When you lie down, you will not be afraid; when you lie down, your sleep will be sweet." Proverbs 3:24

Prayer: Father, I declare Your promise in Proverbs 3:24 over my life. Let my sleep be sweet and free from fear. I cancel every bad dream in the name of Jesus and claim peaceful rest tonight. Amen.

Prayer to Rebuke Fear from Nightmares

Scripture: "For God has not given us a spirit of fear, but of power, love, and a sound mind." 2 Timothy 1:7

Prayer: Lord, I rebuke the spirit of fear that tries to oppress me through bad dreams. As 2 Timothy 1:7 declares, You have given me power, love, and a sound mind. Let Your peace guard my thoughts as I sleep. In Jesus' name, Amen.

Prayer to Break Dream Manipulation

Scripture: "The thief does not come except to steal, and to kill, and to destroy." John 10:10

Prayer: Lord, I stand against the enemy's attempts to steal my peace through bad dreams. As John 10:10 says, You came to give me life abundantly. I cancel every form of dream manipulation in Jesus' name. I declare that my mind is under the covering of the blood of Jesus, and no scheme of the enemy shall prevail against me. I rebuke every spirit of fear, deception, and confusion, and I welcome Your presence to fill my thoughts as I sleep. Let my dreams be filled with Your truth, guidance, and divine revelation. I receive the rest and peace that only You can give, knowing that You watch over me. Thank You, Lord, for Your protection and for surrounding me with Your unfailing love. In Jesus' name, amen.

Prayer for God's Angels to Guard Me

Scripture: "For He will command His angels concerning you to guard you in all your ways." Psalm 91:11

Prayer: Father, I ask You to command Your angels to guard me as I sleep. According to Psalm 91:11, let them surround me and cancel every bad dream sent by the enemy. In Jesus' name, Amen.

Prayer for Deliverance from Evil Dreams

Scripture: "And lead us not into temptation but deliver us from evil." Matthew 6:13

Prayer: I come before You in the name of Jesus Christ, my Savior and Redeemer. Lord, I seek Your divine protection over my mind, my thoughts, and my dreams. Your Word in Philippians 4:7 declares that Your peace, which surpasses all understanding, will guard my heart and mind in Christ Jesus. I ask that You surround me with Your presence and let no evil influence take hold of my thoughts. I take authority over every lie, fear, or deception that tries to infiltrate my mind, and I declare that my thoughts are aligned with Your truth.

Cover me with the blood of Jesus, and let my dreams be filled with Your peace, wisdom, and revelation. Thank You, Lord, for being my refuge and stronghold. I trust in Your power to guard and keep me. In Jesus' name, amen.

Matthew 6:13 teaches us to pray, "Lead us not into temptation, but deliver us from evil." Father, I ask that You guard my heart and mind against every evil influence that seeks to enter my subconscious while I sleep.

By the power of the Holy Spirit, I renounce and reject every scheme of the enemy, every fear, anxiety, and ungodly thought that tries to take root in my mind. Let no weapon formed against me prosper and may every assignment of darkness against my dreams be broken in the mighty name of Jesus.

Lord, I pray that You cleanse my mind and fill it with Your perfect peace, as promised in Isaiah 26:3: "You will keep in perfect peace those whose minds are steadfast, because they trust in You." Let my thoughts be aligned with Your truth, and let my sleep be restful, free from disturbance, and filled with Your presence. I plead the blood of Jesus over my mind, my spirit, and my home. Let Your angels stand guard around me, protecting me from any spiritual attack. May my dreams be a place where You reveal Your wisdom, guidance, and comfort, rather than a battleground for the enemy. I surrender my sleep to You, Lord, trusting in Your unfailing love and power to keep me safe. In Jesus' mighty name, I pray. Amen.

Prayer to Cast Down Imaginations

Scripture: "Casting down imaginations, and every high thing that exalts itself against the knowledge of God." 2 Corinthians 10:5

Prayer: In the name of Jesus, I cast down every negative image and imagination from bad dreams. As 2 Corinthians 10:5 says, I bring every thought captive to the obedience of Christ. Amen.

Prayer for God's Peace Over My Mind

Scripture: "And the peace of God, which transcends all understanding, will guard your hearts and your minds in Christ Jesus." Philippians 4:7

Prayer: Heavenly Father, I come before You in gratitude, acknowledging Your love, power, and faithfulness. Lord, I ask for Your divine peace to settle over me tonight, just as You promised in Philippians 4:7: *"And the peace of God, which surpasses all understanding, will guard your hearts and your minds in Christ Jesus."* Let this peace surround me like a shield, protecting my heart and mind from all fear, worry, and distress.

In the name of Jesus, I cancel and reject every bad dream, every troubling thought, and every attack of the enemy against my rest. I declare that my sleep is covered by the blood of Jesus, and no darkness shall disturb me. Instead of fear, fill my mind with Your truth. Instead of nightmares, let my dreams be filled with Your presence, Your promises, and Your divine guidance.

Lord, I invite Your Holy Spirit to rest upon me and within me. Let my sleep be deep, restful, and restorative, free from any disturbance. May I awaken refreshed, renewed, and filled with Your joy. As I lay down, I trust in Psalm 4:8, which says: *"In peace I will lie down and sleep, for You alone, Lord, make me dwell in safety."* Thank You, Father, for being my refuge and protector. I surrender my night to You, knowing that You are always with me. I rest in Your unfailing love and the assurance of Your presence. In Jesus' mighty name, Amen.

Prayer Against Demonic Attacks

Scripture: "Behold, I have given you authority to tread on serpents and scorpions, and over all the power of the enemy." Luke 10:19

Prayer: Heavenly Father, I come before You in the mighty name of Jesus Christ, my Savior and Deliverer. I thank You for the authority You have given me through Your Word, as Luke 10:19 declares: "Behold, I have given you authority to tread on serpents and scorpions, and over all the power of the enemy, and nothing shall hurt you." Standing on this promise, I take full authority over every scheme, attack, and deception of the enemy that seeks to infiltrate my dreams.

In the name of Jesus, I cancel and nullify every demonic assignment against my mind while I sleep. I rebuke every spirit of fear, torment, confusion, and deception. No weapon formed against me shall prosper, for I am covered by the blood of Jesus (Isaiah 54:17). I declare that my mind is a territory of peace, free from every evil intrusion, because greater is He who is in me than he who is in the world (1 John 4:4).

Lord, I declare my victory in Christ over all the power of the enemy. I proclaim that my dreams will be filled with Your presence, Your voice, and Your divine revelations. Let my sleep be a place of rest, restoration, and communion with You. Instead of fear, I receive faith. Instead of oppression, I receive freedom. Instead of darkness, I welcome Your glorious light. I call upon Your heavenly angels to encamp around me, as promised in Psalm 91:11: "For He will command His angels concerning you to guard you in all your ways." Lord, let no evil come near me, and may Your Holy Spirit fill my room with divine peace. I surrender this night into Your hands, trusting in Your perfect protection. I declare these things in the mighty and victorious name of Jesus Christ. Amen!

Prayer for God's Light to Shine in the Darkness

Scripture: "The light shines in the darkness, and the darkness has not overcome it." John 1:5

Prayer: Lord, let Your light shine in my sleep and dispel all darkness, as John 1:5 proclaims. I cancel every bad dream and declare that darkness will not overcome me. Amen.

Prayer to Cancel Generational Dream Curses

Scripture: "Christ redeemed us from the curse of the law by becoming a curse for us." Galatians 3:13

Prayer: Heavenly Father, I come before You in the mighty name of Jesus Christ, my Lord and Redeemer. I thank You for the power of Your Word and the victory that I have in Christ. Your Word in Galatians 3:13 declares: "Christ redeemed us from the curse of the law by becoming a curse for us, for it is written: 'Cursed is everyone who is hung on a pole.'" Because of Jesus' sacrifice, I declare that I am redeemed from every generational curse, including those that manifest through bad dreams, fear, and torment.

In the name of Jesus, I break and renounce every curse passed down through my bloodline—whether through past sins, idolatry, or spoken words—that seeks to affect my sleep and peace. I declare that I am no longer bound by the sins of my ancestors, for Your Word says in 2 Corinthians 5:17: "If anyone is in Christ, the new creation has come: The old has gone, the new is here!" I stand on this truth and proclaim my freedom in Jesus' name.

Lord, I apply the blood of Jesus over my mind, dreams, and subconscious. I cancel every demonic influence that tries to gain access to my sleep through past generational ties. Every spirit of fear, torment, and oppression is cast out in Jesus' name. I reject every ungodly pattern, and I choose to walk in the fullness of my divine inheritance—one of peace, joy, and righteousness in the Holy Spirit (Romans 14:17).

Father, I ask that You fill my dreams with Your presence. Let Your Holy Spirit purify my mind, removing every lingering effect of generational strongholds. I welcome Your angels to encamp around me, ensuring that no evil enters my sleep. Your Word in Psalm 127:2 promises that You give sleep to Your beloved, and I receive that gift tonight in faith.

Thank You, Lord, for setting me free. I declare that from this moment forward, my sleep will be peaceful, my dreams will be filled with divine revelations, and I will wake up strengthened by Your love. I seal this prayer in the mighty and victorious name of Jesus Christ. Amen

Prayer to Renew My Mind

Scripture: "Do not be conformed to this world but be transformed by the renewal of your mind." Romans 12:2

Prayer: Lord, renew my mind and cleanse it from the effects of bad dreams. Romans 12:2 reminds me that transformation comes through You. Fill my thoughts with Your truth and peace. Amen.

Prayer for the Blood of Jesus to Cover Me

Scripture: "And they overcame him by the blood of the Lamb." Revelation 12:11

Prayer: Lord, I plead the blood of Jesus over my mind and dreams. Revelation 12:11 assures me of victory through the blood. I cancel every negative dream in Jesus' name. Amen.

Prayer for God to Reveal Hidden Threats

Scripture: "Call to Me, and I will answer you, and will tell you great and hidden things." Jeremiah 33

Prayer: Lord, reveal any hidden threats behind my bad dreams, as Jeremiah 33:3 promises. Expose the schemes of the enemy and give me wisdom to pray effectively. Amen.

Prayer for Victory in the Spirit Realm

Scripture: "For the weapons of our warfare are not of the flesh but have divine power to destroy strongholds." 2 Corinthians 10:4

Prayer: Heavenly Father, I come before You in the mighty name of Jesus Christ, my Lord and Savior. I thank You for the authority You have given me through Your Word. As 2 Corinthians 10:4 declares, *"The weapons of our warfare are not carnal, but mighty through God to the pulling down of strongholds."* Lord, I take up these spiritual weapons—Your Word, prayer, the blood of Jesus, and the power of the Holy Spirit—to destroy every stronghold that is causing bad dreams, fear, and spiritual oppression in my sleep.

In the name of Jesus, I tear down and cast out every demonic force that seeks to torment me in my dreams. I reject every lie, deception, and attack of the enemy. No weapon formed against me shall prosper, for I am a child of God, redeemed and protected by the power of the cross (Isaiah 54:17). I cover my mind and subconscious with the blood of Jesus, sealing every entry point against the forces of darkness.

Lord, I declare Your victory over my sleep! I rebuke every spirit of fear, anxiety, and confusion, and I invite Your Holy Spirit to fill my mind with peace and truth. As Ephesians 6:11-12 instructs, I put on the full armor of God, standing firm against the schemes of the enemy. I wield the sword of the Spirit, which is Your Word, declaring that greater is He who is in me than he who is in the world (1 John 4:4).

Tonight, I decree that my dreams will be filled with Your presence, divine revelations, and heavenly peace. No darkness shall enter my sleep, for You, Lord, are my refuge and my fortress (Psalm 91:2). I trust in You to guard my heart and mind and to bless me with restful, undisturbed sleep, as promised in Psalm 4:8: "In peace I will lie down and sleep, for You alone, Lord, make me dwell in safety."

Thank You, Father, for the victory I have in Christ. I rest in the assurance that I am more than a conqueror through Him who loves me (Romans 8:37). I declare that my sleep is covered, my mind is free, and my spirit is victorious. In Jesus' mighty and powerful name, Amen!

Prayer for Restored Peace in Sleep

Scripture: "Come to Me, all who are weary and burdened, and I will give you rest." Matthew 11:28

Prayer: Heavenly Father, I come before You with a heart that longs for Your presence and peace. Your Word in Matthew 11:28 invites me to come to You when I am weary and burdened, and You promise to give me rest. So, Lord, I surrender every worry, every fear, and every troubling thought to You. I lay down every burden that has weighed on my mind, especially those caused by bad dreams and restless nights.

Lord, I ask that You restore my peace and grant me the deep, undisturbed sleep that comes from being in Your care. As Psalm 4:8 declares, "In peace I will lie down and sleep, for You alone, Lord, make me dwell in safety." Surround me with Your divine protection, covering me with the blood of Jesus, and let no evil come near my dwelling (Psalm 91:10-11).

I rebuke every force of darkness that seeks to invade my sleep, and I declare that my mind is a place of peace, purity, and divine revelation. Let my dreams be filled with Your presence, Your Word, and Your guidance. I invite Your Holy Spirit to cleanse my thoughts, removing every trace of fear, anxiety, and oppression. Let my sleep be a time of restoration, healing, and renewal, so that I wake up strengthened, refreshed, and filled with Your joy.

Thank You, Lord, for being my refuge, my comforter, and my source of perfect rest. I trust in Your unfailing love and power to sustain me through the night. I receive Your peace, and I declare that my sleep will be sweet, just as Proverbs 3:24 promises: "When you lie down, you will not be afraid; when you lie down, your sleep will be sweet."

I praise You in advance for the restful sleep and renewed spirit You are granting me. I rest in the assurance of Your presence, knowing that You watch over me. In Jesus' mighty name, Amen.

Prayer for God's Shield Around Me

Scripture: "But You, O Lord, are a shield about me, my glory, and the lifter of my head." Psalm 3:3

Prayer: Father, be a shield around me tonight, as Psalm 3:3 declares. Protect me from every bad dream and lift my spirit with Your presence. Amen.

Prayer Against the Spirit of Torment

Scripture: "There is no fear in love, but perfect love casts out fear." 1 John 4:18

Prayer: Lord, I rebuke the spirit of torment in my dreams. As 1 John 4:18 says, let Your perfect love cast out all fear and bring peace to my heart. Amen.

Prayer for Victory Over Sleep Paralysis

Scripture: "I sought the Lord, and He answered me and delivered me from all my fears." Psalm 34:4

Prayer: Heavenly Father, I come before You in the mighty name of Jesus Christ, my Deliverer and Protector. Lord, You are my refuge and my strength, and I call upon You in my time of need. Your Word in Psalm 34:4 declares, "I sought the Lord, and He answered me; He delivered me from all my fears." Father, I cry out to You now, asking for complete deliverance from sleep paralysis and every fear, anxiety, or spiritual attack that accompanies it.

In the name of Jesus, I renounce and rebuke every force of darkness that tries to oppress me during the night. I declare that no weapon formed against me shall prosper (Isaiah 54:17) and that I am covered by the blood of Jesus, which breaks every chain and cancels every attack of the enemy. I reject every spirit of fear, for You have not given me a spirit of fear, but of power, love, and a sound mind (2 Timothy 1:7).

Tonight, I take authority over my mind, body, and spirit. I decree that my sleep will be restful, undisturbed, and filled with peace. No fear, no paralysis, and no attack of the enemy shall have power over me. Your Word in Romans 8:37 declares that I am more than a conqueror through Christ, and I walk in that victory now.

Thank You, Lord, for hearing my prayer and for delivering me from every fear. I trust in Your protection, and I receive Your perfect peace as I rest tonight. In Jesus' mighty name, Amen!

Prayer for the Mind of Christ

Scripture: "We have the mind of Christ." 1 Corinthians 2:16

Prayer: Lord, I declare that I have the mind of Christ, as 1 Corinthians 2:16 says. Let my thoughts and dreams align with Your truth and cancel every bad dream in Jesus' name. I take authority over every thought that is not of You, and I cast down imaginations and high things that exalt themselves against Your knowledge. Fill my mind with peace, wisdom, and understanding, and let Your truth reign in every area of my life. I declare that my dreams will be a reflection of Your will, bringing comfort, clarity, and revelation. Thank You for guarding my heart and mind and for covering me with Your perfect peace. In Jesus' name, amen.

Prayer to Declare Victory Over the Enemy

Scripture: "Thanks be to God, who gives us the victory through our Lord Jesus Christ." 1 Corinthians 15:57

Prayer: Lord, I thank You for the victory You give through Jesus Christ, as 1 Corinthians 15:57 proclaims. I cancel every bad dream and declare triumph over the enemy in Jesus' name. Amen.

Prayers for Financial Blessing

Prayer for God's Provision

Scripture: "And my God will meet all your needs according to the riches of His glory in Christ Jesus." Philippians 4:19

Prayer: Heavenly Father, I trust in Your promise in Philippians 4:19, which assures me that You will supply all my needs according to Your riches in glory in Christ Jesus. You are my provider, and I declare that lack has no place in my life. I reject fear and anxiety over my finances, knowing that You are faithful to sustain me. Open the doors of provision, Lord, and pour out blessings that I cannot contain. Lead me in wisdom to steward my resources well and to be a blessing to others. Let my life be a testimony of Your abundant goodness and faithfulness. In Jesus' name, Amen.

Prayer for Abundance

Scripture: "The thief comes only to steal and kill and destroy; I have come that they may have life and have it to the full." John 10:10

Prayer: Lord Jesus, I come before You in faith, knowing that You are my provider, my source, and my sustainer. You have promised in John 10:10 that while the enemy comes to steal, kill, and destroy, You have come that I may have life and have it more abundantly. I stand on this promise today, declaring that the enemy has no power over my finances, resources, or blessings in Jesus' name.

I rebuke and cancel every scheme of the enemy designed to bring lack, debt, financial loss, or stress into my life. Your Word in Malachi 3:11 declares that You will rebuke the devourer for my sake, so I claim that promise over my finances now. Every attempt of the enemy to steal my provision is rendered powerless by the authority of Jesus Christ. I trust in You as Jehovah Jireh, my Provider, just as You provided for Abraham (Genesis 22:14). I cast aside all worry, fear, and doubt, for Your Word in Philippians 4:19 promises: *"And my God will meet all your needs according to the riches of His glory in Christ Jesus."* I receive that promise and declare that I lack nothing, for You are my Shepherd (Psalm 23:1).

Thank You, Lord, for blessing me and making me a blessing to others. I declare financial freedom, stability, and prosperity in accordance with Your will. May all that I receive be used to honor You and advance Your kingdom. In Jesus' mighty and victorious name, Amen!

Prayer to Break Financial Strongholds

Scripture: "For the weapons of our warfare are not carnal but mighty in God for pulling down strongholds." 2 Corinthians 10:4

Prayer: Heavenly Father, I come before You in the mighty name of Jesus Christ, my Provider and Deliverer. I thank You for the authority You have given me through Your Word, and I stand firmly in the power of Your promises. Your Word in 2 Corinthians 10:4 declares that *"The weapons of our warfare are not carnal, but mighty through God to the pulling down of strongholds."* Today, I take up these spiritual weapons—prayer, faith, the Word of God, and the blood of Jesus—to pull down every financial stronghold that has been blocking my breakthrough.

In the name of Jesus, I rebuke and cast down every demonic force, generational curse, spirit of lack, delay, and financial oppression that has tried to hinder my prosperity. No weapon formed against my finances shall prosper, and every tongue that rises against me in judgment, I condemn (Isaiah 54:17). The enemy has no right to my resources, my wealth, or my provision, because I am a child of God, redeemed by the blood of the Lamb.

Lord, I declare Your supernatural provision over my life. I stand on Philippians 4:19, which says: *"And my God shall supply all your need according to His riches in glory by Christ Jesus."* I trust that You will meet every need, open every closed door, and release every delayed blessing. I reject the spirit of poverty and declare that I walk in the abundance and overflow of Your kingdom.

Break every financial limitation, Lord! Release divine favor, creative ideas, and financial wisdom that will lead me into prosperity. Let the blessings of Deuteronomy 28:12 manifest in my life: *"The Lord will open to you His good treasury, the heavens, to give the rain to your land in its season and to bless all the work of your hands."* May everything I touch be fruitful and successful according to Your will. Amen.

Prayer for Divine Opportunities

Scripture: "You shall remember the Lord your God, for it is He who gives you power to get wealth." Deuteronomy 8:18

Prayer: Lord, I acknowledge that You are the one who gives me the ability to create wealth, as stated in Deuteronomy 8:18. Open my eyes to divine opportunities and help me steward them wisely. Lord, I ask for Your divine provision to overflow in my life. Open the windows of heaven and pour out a blessing that I cannot contain (Malachi 3:10). Let opportunities, favor, and financial breakthroughs come according to Your perfect will. Fill my life with wisdom in stewardship, so that I may handle my resources in a way that glorifies You. Amen.

Prayer to Cancel Financial Curses

Scripture: "Christ redeemed us from the curse of the law by becoming a curse for us." Galatians 3:13

Prayer: Heavenly Father, I stand on the promise of Deuteronomy 15:6. You have declared that You will bless me as You have promised, and I trust in Your faithfulness. Lord, grant me the wisdom to steward my finances according to Your principles. Teach me to be diligent, to work with integrity, and to make wise investments. Let me not fall into debt or financial bondage but walk in the abundance of Your provision.

Father, I cancel every financial curse operating in my life through the blood of Jesus, as Galatians 3:13 assures me. Every generational curse, every limitation, and every spirit of lack is broken in Jesus' name. I declare freedom from lack and release Your blessings into my finances. I choose to walk in divine abundance, knowing that You are my source and provider.

Help me to be a lender and not a borrower, a giver and not one who lacks. Let my financial decisions align with Your will so that I may be a blessing to others and bring glory to Your name. Open doors of opportunity, and pour out blessings that overflow in my life. I receive Your promise, Lord, and I ask that it manifest fully in every area of my life. In Jesus' name, Amen.

Prayer for Wisdom in Finances

Scripture: "If any of you lacks wisdom, you should ask God, who gives generously to all without finding fault." James 1:5

Prayer: Lord, grant me wisdom in managing my finances, as James 1:5 promises. Help me to make decisions that align with Your will and lead to financial stability and growth. Father, I give my finances over to You, asking that You use them for Your glory and purpose. Let me be a good steward of the blessings You provide, and may I be a blessing to others. I decree and declare that financial freedom, restoration, and increase are my portion, in the mighty name of Jesus Christ! Amen and Amen! Amen.

Prayer for Opened Heaven

Scripture: "The Lord will open the heavens, the storehouse of His bounty, to send rain on your land in season and to bless all the work of your hands." Deuteronomy 28:12

Prayer: Father, I stand on the promise in Deuteronomy 28:12, that You will open the heavens—the storehouse of Your bounty—and send rain on my land in its season. Lord, I ask that You bless all the work of my hands and cause my efforts to prosper. Let the heavens be open over my life, and let the outpouring of Your provision flow into every area where I have been in lack.

Lord, I come against every spiritual barrier that would attempt to block the rain of Your blessing. I cancel any curse, hindrance, or stronghold that seeks to keep me in financial drought. Release Your abundance, O God, and align my life with Your divine favor. Bless the seeds I have sown in faith and cause them to yield an abundant harvest.

Father, I ask for divine opportunities to be revealed, for connections that lead to breakthrough, and for favor in all my financial dealings. Let this be a season of supernatural provision and increase as You open the heavens over me. Empower me to steward the blessings You give me with wisdom and integrity, and use my life as a testimony of Your goodness and faithfulness. In Jesus' name, I pray, Amen.

Prayer for Debt Cancellation

Scripture: "Owe no one anything, except to love each other." Romans 13:8

Prayer: Father, I pray for Your intervention in canceling my debts, as Romans 13:8 encourages. Free me from the burden of debt so I can serve You and others freely. Amen.

Prayer for God's Favor in Finances

Scripture: "Surely, Lord, you bless the righteous; you surround them with your favor as with a shield." Psalm 5:12

Prayer: Lord, surround me with Your favor as Psalm 5:12 declares. Let Your favor open financial doors and opportunities that no one can shut. In Jesus' name, Amen.

Prayer to Reclaim Stolen Finances

Scripture: "I will restore to you the years that the swarming locust has eaten." Joel 2:25

Prayer: Lord, I claim restoration of every financial blessing the enemy has stolen, as Joel 2:25 promises. I trust You to return to me more than I have lost. Amen.

Prayer for Financial Breakthrough

Scripture: "Is anything too hard for the Lord?" Genesis 18:14

Prayer: Lord, I know nothing is too hard for You, as Genesis 18:14 states. I pray for a financial breakthrough that will testify to Your greatness. In Jesus' name, Amen.

Prayer for Prosperity

Scripture: "Beloved, I pray that you may prosper in all things and be in health, just as your soul prospers." 3 John 1:2

Prayer: Father, I thank You for the abundant life You have promised in Your Word. As I declare prosperity over my life, I ask that You bless the work of my hands and multiply my resources. Let every area of my life—financially, spiritually, and emotionally—flourish under Your guidance. Help me to remain faithful in all that I do, trusting in Your provision and timing. May my heart stay aligned with Your will, and may I use my blessings to bring glory to You. In Jesus' name, Amen.

Prayer Against Financial Anxiety

Scripture: "Do not be anxious about anything, but in everything... present your requests to God." Philippians 4:6

Prayer: Lord, I bring my financial concerns before You, as Philippians 4:6 instructs. Replace my anxiety with peace and guide me to trust in Your provision. Amen.

Prayer for God to Supply Seed to Sow

Scripture: "Now He who supplies seed to the sower and bread for food will also supply and increase your store of seed." 2 Corinthians 9:10

Prayer: Father, supply seed for me to sow into Your kingdom, as 2 Corinthians 9:10 promises. Multiply my resources and bring an increase for Your glory. Amen.

Prayer for Freedom from Poverty

Scripture: "The Lord will make you the head, not the tail." Deuteronomy 28:13

Prayer: Lord, I thank You for Your promises of blessing and abundance. I ask You to lift me out of financial struggle and poverty, and to open doors of opportunity for prosperity. According to Your Word in Deuteronomy 28:13, make me the head and not the tail, above and not beneath. Guide me with wisdom in every financial decision I make, and bless my efforts so that I may thrive. Help me to trust in Your provision, knowing that You are faithful to fulfill Your promises. In Jesus' name, Amen.

Prayer for Overflowing Blessings

Scripture: "Give, and it will be given to you. A good measure... will be poured into your lap." Luke 6:38

Prayer: Lord, as I give with a generous heart, I stand on Luke 6:38. Let my giving unlock overflowing blessings that will pour into my life. Amen.

Prayer for Breakthrough in Business

Scripture: "Commit to the Lord whatever you do, and He will establish your plans." Proverbs 16:3

Prayer: Father, I commit my work and business into Your hands, as Proverbs 16:3 instructs. I surrender every plan, decision, and effort to You, trusting that You will direct my steps. Bless the work of my hands and grant me wisdom, integrity, and diligence in all I do. Let my business be a testimony of Your provision and favor. Open doors of opportunity, bring the right connections, and remove any obstacles that hinder success. Establish my plans for financial stability and abundance, so I may be a blessing to others and advance Your kingdom. Amen

Prayer for Peace in Financial Matters

Scripture: "The blessing of the Lord makes rich, and He adds no sorrow with it." Proverbs 10:22

Prayer: Lord, let Your blessing make me rich without sorrow, as Proverbs 10:22 declares. Let peace and contentment accompany every financial breakthrough. Amen.

Prayer for God's Promises to Manifest

Scripture: "For the Lord your God will bless you as He has promised." Deuteronomy 15:6

Prayer: Heavenly Father, I stand on the promise of Deuteronomy 15:6. You have declared that You will bless me as You have promised, and I trust in Your faithfulness. Lord, grant me the wisdom to steward my finances according to Your principles. Teach me to be diligent, to work with integrity, and to make wise investments. Let me not fall into debt or financial bondage but walk in the abundance of Your provision. Help me to be a lender and not a borrower, a giver and not one who lacks. Let my financial decisions align with Your will so that I may be a blessing to others and bring glory to Your name. Open doors of opportunity, and pour out blessings that overflow in my life. I receive Your promise, Lord, and I ask that it manifest fully in every area of my life. In Jesus' name, Amen.

Prayer to Glorify God Through Finances

Scripture: "Whatever you do, do it all for the glory of God." 1 Corinthians 10:31

Prayer: Lord, I pray that my finances will glorify You, as 1 Corinthians 10:31 instructs. May every financial blessing I receive be used in alignment with Your will. Teach me to be a wise steward of the resources You provide, handling them with integrity, generosity, and gratitude. Let my finances not only sustain my needs but also be a source of blessing to others. Guide me in giving, saving, and investing in ways that honor You. Use my financial provision to further Your kingdom, support those in need, and bring glory to Your name.

Prayers to Break Generational Curses

Prayer to Renounce Generational Curses

Scripture: "Christ redeemed us from the curse of the law by becoming a curse for us." Galatians 3:13

Prayer: Heavenly Father, I thank You for redeeming me through the blood of Jesus. According to Galatians 3:13, Christ became a curse for me so I could be set free from every generational curse. I renounce any curse spoken over my family and break its power over my life. I declare that I am no longer bound by these curses because I am redeemed in Christ. In Jesus' name, Amen.

Prayer for Freedom Through the Blood of Jesus

Scripture: "In Him we have redemption through His blood, the forgiveness of sins, in accordance with the riches of God's grace." Ephesians 1:7

Prayer: Lord Jesus, I claim redemption through Your precious blood as declared in Ephesians 1:7. I plead the blood of Jesus over my life and my family line. I declare that the blood of Jesus breaks every chain of bondage, cancels every generational curse, and silences every voice of condemnation. By the power of Your blood, I am cleansed, healed, and set free from every stronghold. I stand on the truth that Your sacrifice has made me whole, and no weapon formed against me or my family shall prosper. Thank You for Your grace, for the freedom You have given me, and for the victory in Your name. I declare that from this moment forward, I walk in the fullness of Your redemption. In Jesus' name, amen.

Prayer to Break Curses of Sickness

Scripture: "He took up our pain and bore our suffering." Isaiah 53:4

Prayer: Father, I break every generational curse of sickness and disease in my family line. Your Word in Isaiah 53:4 declares that Jesus took up our pain and bore our suffering. I declare healing and restoration over my body and my descendants. In Jesus' name, Amen.

Prayer to Cancel Curses of Poverty

Scripture: "The blessing of the Lord makes rich, and He adds no sorrow with it." Proverbs 10:22

Prayer: I stand on Your Word and declare freedom over my family line. I cancel every generational curse of poverty, and I break the chains of lack and limitation that have held us captive. I speak Your blessings over my life, as Proverbs 10:22 promises—Your blessing brings wealth without sorrow. May Your divine provision flow freely into our lives, and may every member of my family walk in financial freedom, abundance, and peace. Let this be a new season of prosperity and favor, rooted in Your grace. In Jesus' name, Amen.

Prayer to Break Curses of Idolatry

Scripture: "You shall have no other gods before Me." Exodus 20

Prayer: Father, I repent for any idolatry in my family line, as Exodus 20:3 commands. I break every curse caused by the worship of false gods or idols. I declare that my family will serve You alone, the true and living God. In Jesus' name, Amen.

Prayer for Generational Healing

Scripture: "I will restore to you the years that the swarming locust has eaten." Joel 2:25

Prayer: Lord, I come before You in faith, asking for Your restoration in my family, as You promised in Joel 2:25. Heal the wounds caused by generational curses, and restore the blessings that have been lost. I declare that every area of brokenness in my family will be made whole by Your healing power. Bring peace where there has been conflict, unity where there has been division, and restoration where there has been loss. I believe that You are a God of second chances, and I trust that my family will walk in healing, wholeness, and Your divine favor. In Jesus' name, Amen.

Prayer to Renounce Curses of Fear

Scripture: "For God has not given us a spirit of fear, but of power, love, and a sound mind." 2 Timothy 1:7

Prayer: Father, I renounce every generational curse of fear and anxiety. According to 2 Timothy 1:7, You have not given me a spirit of fear, but of power, love, and a sound mind. I declare that fear has no hold over me or my family. Amen.

Prayer to Break Curses of Rebellion

Scripture: "If you are willing and obedient, you will eat the good things of the land." Isaiah 1:19

Prayer: Lord, I repent of any rebellion in my family line. I break every curse that has resulted from disobedience. Your Word in Isaiah 1:19 says that obedience leads to blessing, and I declare that my family will walk in obedience to You. Amen.

Prayer Against Generational Addictions

Scripture: "So if the Son sets you free, you will be free indeed." John 8:36

Prayer: Lord Jesus, I stand on John 8:36, declaring that whom the Son sets free is free indeed. I break every curse of addiction in my family line—whether physical, emotional, or spiritual. Every stronghold that has kept my family bound, I command it to be shattered in Jesus' name. Let Your deliverance, healing, and restoration flow through every generation. Fill the void left by addiction with Your love, peace, and purpose. I declare total freedom, renewed minds, and transformed hearts for myself and my family. In Jesus' name, Amen.

Prayer to Break Curses of Division

Scripture: "How good and pleasant it is when God's people live together in unity!" Psalm 133:1

Prayer: Father, I break every generational curse of division and strife in my family. Psalm 133:1 speaks of the blessing of unity, and I declare that over my household. Bring restoration and peace to my family. Amen.

Prayer to Cancel Curses of Witchcraft

Scripture: "No weapon formed against you shall prosper." Isaiah 54:17

Prayer: Lord, I cancel every curse of witchcraft that has affected my family. Isaiah 54:17 declares that no weapon formed against me shall prosper. I stand in the victory of Your Word and declare freedom from all demonic oppression, manipulation, and control. I bind every evil spirit and decree that it has no power over my life or my family. I claim the protection of Your angels, and I cover myself and my loved ones with the blood of Jesus. Let Your truth break every chain, and let Your light expose and dispel every darkness. I declare that we are free, redeemed, and victorious in You. Thank You, Lord, for Your divine protection and for the power of Your deliverance. In Jesus' name, Amen.

Prayer to Break Curses of Barrenness

Scripture: "He gives the barren woman a home, making her the joyous mother of children." Psalm 113:9

Prayer: Lord, I come before You, standing on Psalm 113:9, which declares that You give the barren woman a home and make her a joyful mother of children. I break every curse of barrenness in my family line, whether physical, spiritual, or emotional. I declare fruitfulness, blessing, and life over my household. Let every area of lack be filled with abundance according to Your divine will. May our lineage flourish under Your favor, and may every delayed promise be fulfilled in Your perfect timing. In Jesus' name, Amen.

Prayer for Freedom from Generational Sin

Scripture: "If we confess our sins, He is faithful and just to forgive us our sins and to cleanse us." 1 John 1:9

Prayer: Father, I confess the sins of my ancestors and my own. According to 1 John 1:9, You are faithful to forgive and cleanse us. Break every curse caused by generational sin and wash us in Your righteousness. Amen.

Prayer to Break Curses of Anger

Scripture: "Refrain from anger, and forsake wrath." Psalm 37:8

Prayer: Lord, I break every generational curse of anger and rage. Psalm 37:8 reminds us to forsake anger. I declare peace and self-control over my family line. Amen.

Prayer to Break Curses of Unforgiveness

Scripture: "Forgive, and you will be forgiven." Luke 6:37

Prayer: Lord, I break every generational curse caused by unforgiveness. As Luke 6:37 instructs, I choose to forgive, and I ask for forgiveness for my family. Release us from this bondage and bring healing. Amen.

Prayer to Break Word Curses

Scripture: "The tongue has the power of life and death." Proverbs 18:21

Prayer: Father, I cancel every negative word spoken over my family, for Proverbs 18:21 declares that the tongue has the power of life and death. I reject every curse, every word of doubt, and every harmful declaration that has taken root in our lives. Instead, I speak life, blessing, and favor into my family line. Let Your promises be established in us, and may our words align with Your truth. Fill our mouths with declarations of faith, love, and victory. In Jesus' name, Amen.

Prayer Against Generational Pride

Scripture: "God opposes the proud but gives grace to the humble." James 4:6

Prayer: Lord, I break every generational curse of pride and arrogance that has hindered my family. Your Word in James 4:6 declares that You resist the proud but give grace to the humble. I surrender my heart and my family's lineage to You, asking that You replace pride with a spirit of humility, teachability, and grace. Let us walk in the humility of Christ, seeking to serve rather than be served. Transform our hearts and renew our minds so that we may reflect Your love and wisdom in all we do. In Jesus' name, Amen.

Prayer to Break Curses of Depression

Scripture: "The joy of the Lord is your strength." Nehemiah 8:10

Prayer: Lord, I stand on Nehemiah 8:10, declaring that Your joy is my strength. I break every generational curse of depression and hopelessness that has weighed down my family. I reject every spirit of heaviness and despair, and I invite Your light, peace, and restoration into our hearts and minds. Let the joy of the Lord overflow in our lives, replacing sorrow with praise, fear with faith, and mourning with dancing. I declare that hope will rise, and peace will reign over my family for generations to come. In Jesus' name, Amen.

Prayer to Break Curses of Failure

Scripture: "You shall be the head and not the tail." Deuteronomy 28:13

Prayer: Father, I cancel every generational curse of failure. Deuteronomy 28:13 promises that I will be the head and not the tail. I declare success and prosperity in every area of my life spiritually, emotionally, financially, and physically. I speak blessings over my family, my work, and my future, knowing that You have destined me for greatness. Break every chain of limitation and release me into the fullness of Your purpose. I declare that Your favor surrounds me, and Your plans for me are for good. Thank You for Your promises that are faithful and true. In Jesus' name, Amen.

Prayer for Generational Blessings

Scripture: "The Lord bless you and keep you; the Lord make His face shine on you." Numbers 6:24-25

Prayer: Lord, I replace every curse with Your blessing, as Numbers 6:24-25 proclaims. Bless and keep my family, and let Your face shine upon us for generations to come. I declare Your peace, favor, and protection over every member of my household. Let Your presence guide us, Your love sustain us, and Your wisdom direct our steps. I speak prosperity, health, and divine favor over our lives, knowing that Your promises are yes and amen. May Your blessings overflow in every area, and may Your glory be evident in our lives for all generations. Thank You, Lord, for Your faithfulness and for the blessing You have promised to those who walk in Your ways. In Jesus' name, Amen.

Prayers to Divorce Spirit Spouses and Anti-Marriage Spirits

Prayer to Renounce Spirit Spouses

Scripture: "Submit yourselves, then, to God. Resist the devil, and he will flee from you." James 4:7

Prayer: Heavenly Father, I submit myself to You completely, surrendering every area of my life under Your authority. I renounce and reject every spirit spouse that has gained access to my life through dreams, generational ties, or past agreements. By the power of the blood of Jesus, I break every covenant, oath, or connection whether knowingly or unknowingly made. As James 4:7 declares, I resist this spirit in Jesus' name, and I command it to flee from me now. Let every chain be shattered, every legal right be revoked, and every doorway be permanently shut. I declare my body, soul, and spirit belong to Christ alone. Thank You, Lord, for my freedom and restoration. In Jesus' mighty name, Amen.

Prayer to Break Ungodly Covenants

Scripture: "Do two walk together unless they have agreed to do so?" Amos 3

Prayer: Father, I break every ungodly covenant or agreement that has been made with spirit spouses. Your Word in Amos 3:3 says that agreement is necessary to walk together. I declare that I will no longer walk in agreement with these spirits. I am free in Jesus' name. Amen.

Prayer to Destroy Spiritual Marriages

Scripture: "What therefore God has joined together, let not man separate." Mark 10:9

Prayer: Lord, I declare that no spiritual marriage created by the enemy has any authority over my life. Your Word in Mark 10:9 speaks of marriages ordained by You, and I declare that only Your plans for my relationships will stand. I annul every demonic union in Jesus' name. Amen.

Prayer Against Anti-Marriage Spirits

Scripture: "The thief comes only to steal and kill and destroy; I have come that they may have life, and have it to the full." John 10:10

Prayer: Father, I come against every anti-marriage spirit that seeks to destroy Your plan for my relationships. As John 10:10 declares, Jesus came to give me life to the fullest. I cancel every attack on my marriage and relationships in Jesus' name. Amen.

Prayer for Deliverance from Dreams

Scripture: "For God has not given us a spirit of fear, but of power and of love and of a sound mind." 2 Timothy 1:7

Prayer: Lord, I cancel every demonic dream involving spirit spouses or anti-marriage spirits. I refuse to entertain these dreams, and I declare 2 Timothy 1:7 over my life. I receive Your power, love, and sound mind. Amen.

Prayer to Sever Generational Links

Scripture: "You shall not bow down to them or serve them, for I the Lord your God am a jealous God, visiting the iniquity of the fathers on the children to the third and the fourth generation." Exodus 20:5

Prayer: Lord, I repent for the sins of my ancestors that may have opened doors to spirit spouses. I declare that every generational link is severed by the blood of Jesus. I refuse to be bound by these curses, in Jesus' name. Amen.

Prayer to Close Spiritual Doors

Scripture: "Behold, I have set before you an open door, which no one is able to shut." Revelation 3:8

Prayer: Father, I close every spiritual door that was opened to spirit spouses or anti-marriage spirits. Only the doors You have opened for me will remain. I seal every door with the blood of Jesus. Amen.

Prayer to Break Demonic Assignments

Scripture: "No weapon formed against you shall prosper." Isaiah 54:17

Prayer: Lord, I declare that no weapon formed against my marital destiny will prosper. Every assignment of spirit spouses or anti-marriage spirits is canceled. I walk in victory, according to Isaiah 54:17. Amen.

Prayer for the Power of the Cross

Scripture: "Having disarmed principalities and powers, He made a public spectacle of them, triumphing over them in it." Colossians 2:15

Prayer: Jesus, I declare Your victory over every spirit spouse and anti-marriage spirit. You have disarmed principalities and powers, and I claim that triumph over my life. Thank You for setting me free. Amen.

Prayer for the Purity of the Body

Scripture: "Do you not know that your bodies are temples of the Holy Spirit?" 1 Corinthians 6:19

Prayer: Father, my body is the temple of the Holy Spirit, as declared in 1 Corinthians 6:19. I cleanse my body from every spiritual contamination caused by spirit spouses. I dedicate myself to You alone. Amen.

Prayer to Break Soul Ties

Scripture: "Flee from sexual immorality." 1 Corinthians 6:18

Prayer: Lord, I break every soul tie with spirit spouses and cancel their influence over my life. I flee from every form of spiritual immorality and choose purity in Jesus' name. Amen.

Prayer to Invoke Angelic Assistance

Scripture: "Are not all angels ministering spirits sent to serve those who will inherit salvation?" Hebrews 1:14

Prayer: Father, I ask for Your angels to war on my behalf. Let them fight against every spirit spouse and anti-marriage spirit, as Hebrews 1:14 promises their help. I am victorious in Christ. Amen.

Prayer to Protect My Mind

Scripture: "We take captive every thought to make it obedient to Christ." 2 Corinthians 10:5

Prayer: Lord, I take captive every thought and imagination planted by spirit spouses. I make them obedient to Christ, as 2 Corinthians 10:5 instructs. Fill my mind with Your truth. Remove every lie and deception that has taken root in my heart, and let Your Word be the foundation on which my thoughts stand.

I reject every negative influence, every oppressive spirit, and every attempt to disrupt the peace and purity of my mind. I declare that my thoughts belong to You alone, and I choose to focus on what is pure, lovely, and of good report, as Philippians 4:8 teaches. Lord, I invite Your Holy Spirit to cleanse my mind, renewing me from the inside out. Break every chain of unhealthy attachments, bring healing where wounds have caused confusion, and restore my soul.

Empower me to walk in Your victory, to live in Your freedom, and to stand firm in the truth of who I am in Christ. May Your peace guard my heart and mind, and may Your love fill every part of my being. In Jesus' name, I pray. Amen.

Prayer for Restored Relationships

Scripture: "What God has joined together, let no one separate." Matthew 19:6

Prayer: Father, restore every relationship that has been damaged by anti-marriage spirits. As Matthew 19:6 declares, what You have joined together, let no one separate. Bring healing and unity to my relationships. Amen.

Prayer to Declare Victory in Jesus

Scripture: "They triumphed over him by the blood of the Lamb and by the word of their testimony." Revelation 12:11

Prayer: Lord, I declare victory over spirit spouses and anti-marriage spirits by the blood of the Lamb and the word of my testimony. I am free because of Your sacrifice. I proclaim that every chain that has held me captive is broken, every lie and distortion that has been planted in my life is uprooted by the power of Your truth. In the name of Jesus, I stand firm, knowing that Your blood has set me free from every oppressive spirit and every hindrance to my divine purpose. I renounce any agreement made knowingly or unknowingly with these spirits, and I break every ungodly covenant that has been established in my life. I declare that my destiny is not shaped by the lies of the enemy, but by the truth of Your Word. I receive the fullness of Your healing, restoration, and freedom, knowing that through You, I am whole and complete. Lord, I ask for Your protection over my heart, mind, and future, and I thank You that Your plan for me is one of hope, peace, and godly relationships. I trust that Your will for my life is unfolding in perfect timing, and I stand in faith, knowing that no weapon formed against me shall prosper. Thank You, Jesus, for the victory You have won on the cross. I am free, and I am more than a conqueror through You. Amen.

Prayer to Cancel Spiritual Marital Claims

Scripture: "If anyone is in Christ, the new creation has come: The old has gone, the new is here!" 2 Corinthians 5:17

Prayer: Father, I come before You in the name of Jesus, declaring that I am a new creation in Christ. According to 2 Corinthians 5:17, the old has passed away, and the new has come. Therefore, I reject and cancel every spiritual marital claim made over my life. Any covenant, pact, or agreement that I or my ancestors unknowingly or knowingly entered into with spirit spouses is now nullified by the blood of Jesus. I declare that the blood of Jesus breaks every legal right these spirits have over me. I belong to You, Lord, and I dedicate my body, soul, and spirit to Your holy purpose. In Jesus' name, I declare that I am free from every spiritual bondage. Amen.

Prayer to Reverse Curses

Scripture: "Christ redeemed us from the curse of the law by becoming a curse for us, for it is written: 'Cursed is everyone who is hung on a pole.'" Galatians 3:13

Prayer: Lord Jesus, I thank You for redeeming me from the curse of the law by becoming a curse for me on the cross, as Galatians 3:13 declares. Today, I reverse every curse placed on my relationships, marriage, or future marriage by spirit spouses or anti-marriage spirits. I decree that the power of these curses is broken because of the finished work of the cross. Every word spoken, ritual performed, or spiritual transaction made against me is canceled by the authority of Jesus Christ. I ask for Your blessings, favor, and restoration to replace these curses. In Jesus' mighty name, I declare that I am no longer under the control or influence of these spirits. I walk in freedom and victory. Amen.

Prayer to Break Chains of Bondage

Scripture: "The Spirit of the Lord is on me, because He has anointed me to proclaim good news to the poor. He has sent me to proclaim freedom for the captives and recovery of sight for the blind, to set the oppressed free." Luke 4:18

Prayer: Father, I thank You for sending Jesus, who declared in Luke 4:18 that He came to set the oppressed free. Today, I claim the freedom that Jesus purchased for me through His sacrifice. Every chain of bondage created by spirit spouses, anti-marriage spirits, or demonic forces is broken in Jesus' name. I declare that I am no longer a captive to their lies, manipulations, or attacks. I bind every spirit that has oppressed my marital destiny and command it to leave my life now. Holy Spirit, fill me with Your peace and power, and help me walk in the freedom that Christ has provided. I decree that my future is secure in You, Lord, and that no weapon formed against my relationships will prosper. Amen.

Prayer for Divine Alignment

Scripture: "For I know the plans I have for you, declares the Lord, plans to prosper you and not to harm you, plans to give you hope and a future." Jeremiah 29:11

Prayer: Heavenly Father, I stand on the promise of Jeremiah 29:11, knowing that You have good plans for my life. I declare that my relationships, marriage, and future are aligned with

Your divine purpose. Every plan of spirit spouses or anti-marriage spirits to derail or delay my destiny is canceled in the name of Jesus. I bind and cast out any spirit that has sought to hinder Your blessings in my life. Lord, I submit to Your will and trust in Your perfect timing for my relationships. I pray for divine alignment with the partner You have chosen for me, and I declare that no demonic interference will disrupt what You have ordained. I thank You for Your faithfulness and the assurance of a hopeful future. Amen.

Prayer to Walk in Dominion

Scripture: "I have given you authority to trample on snakes and scorpions and to overcome all the power of the enemy; nothing will harm you." Luke 10:19

Prayer: Lord Jesus, I thank You for giving me authority to trample on snakes and scorpions and to overcome all the power of the enemy, as You declared in Luke 10:19. Today, I rise in that authority to take dominion over every spirit spouse and anti-marriage spirit operating in my life. I declare that these spirits have no power over me, and I command them to leave in Jesus' name. By the power of the Holy Spirit, I destroy every altar, chain, or bond that has tied me to these spirits. I decree that I will walk in the freedom, dominion, and authority that You have given me as a child of God. Nothing will harm me, and no plan of the enemy will succeed against me. I walk in victory, proclaiming Your name, Jesus, as my defender and deliverer. Amen.

Prayers Against Demonic Attacks

Prayer for Strength in Battle

Scripture: "Finally, be strong in the Lord and in His mighty power. Put on the full armor of God so that you can take your stand against the devil's schemes." Ephesians 6:10-11

Prayer: Heavenly Father, I come before You in the name of Jesus, asking for strength in this spiritual battle. Your Word in Ephesians 6:10-11 reminds me to stand strong in Your power and put on the full armor of God to resist the schemes of the enemy. I ask for Your strength to overcome every demonic attack against my mind, body, and spirit. Help me to stand firm, knowing that You are with me, fighting for me. In Jesus' name, Amen.

Prayer to Bind the Enemy

Scripture: "Truly I tell you, whatever you bind on earth will be bound in heaven, and whatever you loose on earth will be loosed in heaven." (Matthew 18:18)

Prayer: Lord, I take the authority given to me in Matthew 18:18, and I bind every demonic spirit and assignment sent against me. I loose Your peace, protection, and power over my life. I declare that no weapon formed against me shall prosper, and I rebuke every plan of the enemy in Jesus' name. Amen.

Prayer for the Blood of Jesus

Scripture: "They triumphed over him by the blood of the Lamb and by the word of their testimony." Revelation 12:11

Prayer: Father, I plead the blood of Jesus over my life, my family, and everything that concerns me. Revelation 12:11 declares that we overcome the enemy by the blood of the Lamb and the word of our testimony. I declare that the blood of Jesus covers and protects me from every demonic attack. In Jesus' name, Amen.

Prayer to Cancel Evil Assignments

Scripture: "No weapon formed against you shall prosper, and every tongue which rises against you in judgment you shall condemn." Isaiah 54:17

Prayer: Lord, I come before You with a heart full of gratitude for the victory that is mine in Christ Jesus. According to Your Word in Isaiah 54:17, "No weapon that is formed against you shall prosper, and every tongue that shall rise against you in judgment you shall condemn." I stand on this promise today, and I cancel every evil assignment, plan, and weapon formed against me. I declare that they will not succeed, for I am covered by the blood of Jesus and shielded by Your mighty power. I condemn every demonic word spoken against me, every plot and strategy of the enemy designed to cause harm, confusion, or destruction in my life. I break the power of every curse, every lie, and every attack. I speak destruction over every evil plan and declare that they will return to the enemy. I stand firm in Your victory, knowing that You have already defeated the powers of darkness on the cross (Colossians 2:15). Lord,

I declare that no weapon, no attack, no curse, and no scheme formed against me shall prevail. I rise above every situation because I am more than a conqueror through Him who loves me (Romans 8:37). I trust in Your protection, Your provision, and Your promises. I claim the victory that You have already won for me and declare that Your peace, joy, and favor will fill every area of my life. I stand in Your victory and boldly declare that Your promises are true. You are my refuge and fortress, and in You, I am safe (Psalm 91:2). Thank You for fighting for me and for the assurance that the enemy's plans are already defeated. I give You all the glory, honor, and praise. In Jesus' name, Amen

Prayer for Protection

Scripture: "The Lord will fight for you; you need only to be still." Exodus 14:14

Prayer: Father, I trust in Your promise in Exodus 14:14 that You fight for me. I call on Your mighty power to protect me from every attack of the enemy. Guard my heart, mind, and soul, and give me peace as I trust in You. In Jesus' name, Amen.

Prayer to Break Strongholds

Scripture: "For the weapons of our warfare are not carnal but mighty in God for pulling down strongholds." 2 Corinthians 10:4

Prayer: Lord, I come against every stronghold in my life. According to 2 Corinthians 10:4, the weapons You have given me are mighty to destroy strongholds. I tear down every demonic stronghold, lie, or oppression in Jesus' name. I declare freedom and victory through Your power. Amen.

Prayer for Angelic Assistance

Scripture: "For He will command His angels concerning you to guard you in all your ways." Psalm 91:11

Prayer: Lord, I ask for Your angels to surround me and guard me against every demonic attack. As promised in Psalm 91:11, You send Your angels to protect those who trust in You. I declare that no evil shall come near me because of Your divine protection. In Jesus' name, Amen.

Prayer to Rebuke Fear

Scripture: "For God has not given us a spirit of fear, but of power and of love and of a sound mind." 2 Timothy 1:7

Prayer: Heavenly Father, I reject the spirit of fear sent by the enemy. Your Word in 2 Timothy 1:7 declares that You have given me power, love, and a sound mind. I rebuke fear, anxiety, and torment, and I declare peace over my heart and mind. In Jesus' name, Amen.

Prayer for Victory in Christ

Scripture: "But thanks be to God, who gives us the victory through our Lord Jesus Christ." 1 Corinthians 15:57

Prayer: Lord, I thank You for the victory You have already given me through Jesus Christ. I stand on the truth of 1 Corinthians 15:57, knowing that I am more than a conqueror.

Every demonic attack must bow to the name of Jesus. I declare that the power of the enemy is defeated, and every stronghold is brought down under the authority of Christ. Thank You, Lord, that through Your sacrifice, I have been made more than an overcomer, and I walk in the freedom that You have purchased for me. I claim Your promises over my life, knowing that no weapon formed against me shall prosper, and every tongue that rises in judgment shall be condemned. Lord, I pray that Your mighty presence will surround me, shield me, and protect me from all forms of spiritual warfare. I ask for Your strength to stand firm, to resist the enemy, and to remain rooted in Your Word. May Your peace guard my heart and mind, and may Your love be my refuge. I declare that the victory is already won, and I walk in that truth, fully confident in Your power and grace. I give You all the glory, honor, and praise, knowing that I am victorious in Christ Jesus. Amen.

Prayer for Deliverance

Scripture: "And call upon me in the day of trouble; I will deliver you, and you will honor me." Psalm 50:15

Prayer: Father, I call on You in this day of trouble. Psalm 50:15 promises that when I call upon You, You will deliver me. I trust in Your power to rescue me from every demonic attack and bring me into a place of peace and safety. Lord, I stand firm on Your Word, knowing that You are my refuge and strength, a very present help in times of trouble.

I ask You to surround me with Your angels, to shield me with Your divine protection, and to silence every voice of fear and confusion that seeks to overwhelm me. I place my trust in Your unfailing love, knowing that no weapon formed against me shall prosper. I claim Your victory over every attack, every lie, and every form of oppression, and I believe that You are working on my behalf, even when I cannot see it.

Father, I surrender this battle to You, knowing that the fight belongs to You and that You will always deliver me. I thank You in advance for the peace You will restore to my heart and the safety You will provide for my life. In Jesus' name, I pray. Amen.

Prayer for Peace

Scripture: "Peace I leave with you; my peace I give you." John 14:27

Prayer: Lord, I declare Your peace over my life. In John 14:27, You promised to leave us with peace that surpasses all understanding. I rebuke every spirit of confusion and chaos sent by the enemy, and I rest in Your peace. In Jesus' name, Amen.

Prayer Against Witchcraft

Scripture: "No one will be able to stand against you all the days of your life." Joshua 1:5

Prayer: Father, I cancel every curse, hex, and spell sent against me. Joshua 1:5 declares that no one can stand against me because You are with me. I break every work of witchcraft by the power of Jesus' name. I renounce every form of dark influence, every assignment of the enemy aimed at my life, and every weapon formed against me, knowing that You are my protector and deliverer. I declare that Your Word is my shield and fortress. I stand firm in the truth that no power of darkness can prevail against the power of Your light. By the blood of Jesus, I render powerless every curse, every spoken word, and every demonic plot designed to harm me. I invite Your Holy Spirit to fill me with peace, strength, and courage, knowing that You are with me wherever I go. I trust in Your authority and believe that You are greater than any force that seeks to oppose me. Lord, I thank You for the victory that is mine through Christ Jesus. I walk in Your protection, free from every attack and every chain of the enemy. Your presence is my security, and Your power is my victory. In Jesus' name, I pray. Amen.

Prayer to Walk in Authority

Scripture: "I have given you authority to trample on snakes and scorpions and to overcome all the power of the enemy." Luke 10:19

Prayer: Lord, I walk in the authority You have given me in Luke 10:19, which says, "Behold, I have given you authority to tread on serpents and scorpions, and over all the power of the enemy, and nothing shall hurt you." I thank You for the power and authority You have entrusted to me through Jesus Christ. I declare, in Your name, that every serpent, scorpion, and attack of the enemy is under my feet. I trample on every demonic force, every spirit of fear, oppression, confusion, and deception. I bind every spirit of infirmity, sickness, and poverty that tries to come against me. In the mighty name of Jesus, I speak destruction over the works of darkness, for I know that no weapon formed against me shall prosper (Isaiah 54:17). I declare that the enemy has no power over me, my family, or my destiny. I stand firm, clothed in Your armor, knowing that You are my protector and my strong tower. I declare victory in every area of my life, for Your Word says in 1 John 4:4, "He who is in me is greater than he who is in the world." I thank You, Father, for the Holy Spirit who empowers me to overcome every challenge and every attack.

Prayer for the Sword of the Spirit

Scripture: "Take the sword of the Spirit, which is the word of God." Ephesians 6:17

Prayer: Lord, I take up the sword of the Spirit tonight. I declare Your Word over my life and use it to fight against every lie of the enemy. Ephesians 6:17 reminds me that Your Word is my weapon, and I declare victory through it. Amen.

Prayer to Stand Firm

Scripture: "Submit yourselves, then, to God. Resist the devil, and he will flee from you." James 4:7

Prayer: Father, I submit myself fully to You and resist every attack of the enemy. As James 4:7 promises, the devil must flee from me when I stand in Your authority. I declare that I am untouchable under Your covering. Amen.

Prayer for a Hedge of Protection

Scripture: "Have You not put a hedge around him and his household and everything he has?" Job 1:10

Prayer: Lord, just as You placed a hedge of protection around Job, I ask for that same hedge to surround me, my family, and all that belongs to me. Job 1:10 reminds me of Your divine protection, and I claim it now. I declare that no demonic attack can penetrate the barrier of Your love and power. Place angels to guard and watch over me. In Jesus' name, Amen.

Prayer to Break Generational Curses

Scripture: "Christ redeemed us from the curse of the law by becoming a curse for us." Galatians 3:13

Prayer: Lord, I stand on the truth of Galatians 3:13 that Christ redeemed me from the curse of the law. I break every generational curse and demonic pattern that has been passed down in my bloodline. I declare freedom in Jesus' name and claim the blessings of Abraham over my life. Amen.

Prayer for Rest and Protection

Scripture: "In peace I will lie down and sleep, for You alone, Lord, make me dwell in safety." Psalm 4:8

Prayer: Father, as I prepare to rest, I trust in Your Word in Psalm 4:8. You alone make me dwell in safety. I command every demonic spirit that seeks to disturb my rest to flee in the name of Jesus. Surround me with Your presence and give me peace. Amen.

Prayer to Rebuke Satan

Scripture: "The Lord rebuke you, Satan!" Zechariah 3:2

Prayer: Lord, I stand in agreement with Your Word in Zechariah 3:2. The Lord rebuke you, Satan! You have no power or place in my life. I command every demonic force to flee now in Jesus' name. I am covered by the blood of Jesus and hidden in Christ. Amen.

Prayer for Total Deliverance

Scripture: "If the Son sets you free, you will be free indeed." John 8:36

Prayer: Jesus, I thank You for the freedom You give. John 8:36 declares that if You set me free, I am free indeed. I declare complete freedom from every demonic attack, chain, and oppression. I am delivered, victorious, and at peace because of You. Let Your power and presence fill my life. In Jesus' name, Amen.

Prayer Against Witchcraft and Evil Forces

Scripture: "No one will be able to stand against you all the days of your life. As I was with Moses, so I will be with you; I will never leave you nor forsake you." Joshua 1:5

Prayer: Heavenly Father, I come before You in the name of Jesus, declaring that no force of witchcraft or evil can stand against me, for You have promised in Joshua 1:5 that You will never leave me nor forsake me. I call upon the power of Your Holy Spirit to destroy every evil plot, incantation, or spell designed to harm me or my family. By the authority given to me in Christ, I break every chain of witchcraft, every spoken curse, and every ritual performed against my life. Let every wicked altar erected in the spiritual realm on my behalf be consumed by Your holy fire. Lord, surround me with Your light, and let the enemy flee from Your presence. I decree that Your presence is my shield, and I am untouchable because You fight for me. In the mighty name of Jesus, I declare victory and freedom from all forms of witchcraft. Amen.

Prayer to Walk Fully in Authority

Scripture: "I have given you authority to trample on snakes and scorpions and to overcome all the power of the enemy; nothing will harm you." Luke 10:19

Prayer: Lord Jesus, I thank You for the authority You have given me to trample on snakes, scorpions, and all the power of the enemy, as You declare in Luke 10:19. Today, I stand boldly in that authority and declare that nothing the enemy tries will harm me. I bind every demonic force, every attack, and every plan formed against me, and I render them powerless in the name of Jesus. Let Your Holy Spirit empower me to walk in this authority daily, understanding that I am a child of the Most High God. Lord, strengthen my faith and give me the confidence to speak Your Word boldly against the enemy's schemes. I declare that through Your power, every stronghold of fear, doubt, and oppression is broken. I claim my victory in Jesus' name and proclaim that I walk fully as a conqueror through Christ. Amen.

Prayer to Wield the Sword of the Spirit

Scripture: "For the word of God is alive and active. Sharper than any double-edged sword, it penetrates even to dividing soul and spirit, joints and marrow; it judges the thoughts and attitudes of the heart." Hebrews 4:12

Prayer: Lord God, I thank You for the power of Your Word, which is alive and active as stated in Hebrews 4:12. I take up the Sword of the Spirit tonight and use it as my weapon against the enemy. Every demonic attack, every lie, and every spirit of confusion must bow to the authority of Your Word. Father, teach me to meditate on Scripture and declare it boldly against the forces of darkness. Let Your Word penetrate my heart and mind, strengthening me for battle. I declare that no power of the enemy can stand against the truth of Your promises. I speak forth Your Word over my life, proclaiming that I am victorious, redeemed, and protected. Lord, let Your Word go forth like a consuming fire, destroying every plan of the wicked one. In the mighty name of Jesus, I declare total victory through the Sword of the Spirit. Amen.

Prayer to Break Generational Curses and Ancestral Chains

Scripture: "Christ redeemed us from the curse of the law by becoming a curse for us, for it is written: 'Cursed is everyone who is hung on a pole.'" Galatians 3:13

Prayer: Lord Jesus, I thank You for redeeming me from every curse of the law, as Galatians 3:13 declares. I bring before You every generational curse, ancestral bondage, and inherited sin that has impacted my life or my family. In Your name, I break every chain of addiction, poverty, sickness, and failure that has been passed down through my bloodline. Lord, I declare that these curses have no power over me because You took my place on the cross and became a curse for me. I plead the blood of Jesus over my life and my family, and I sever every connection to ungodly covenants, pacts, or agreements made by my ancestors. I decree that my lineage is now rooted in Christ and blessed with His promises. Father, renew my family tree and establish us as a generation that serves You wholeheartedly. Thank You for setting me free and making me a new creation. In Jesus' name, Amen.

Prayer for Divine Rest and Protection

Scripture: "In peace I will lie down and sleep, for You alone, Lord, make me dwell in safety." Psalm 4:8

Prayer: Heavenly Father, I thank You for the gift of peace You promise in Psalm 4:8. As I prepare to rest, I ask for Your divine protection over me, my family, and my home. Lord, I declare that no demonic spirit, nightmare, or attack will disturb my rest, for I am hidden in You. Surround me with Your holy angels, and let their presence fill my home with light and peace. I rebuke every spirit of fear, oppression, or torment that seeks to come against me. Let Your perfect peace guard my heart and mind, silencing every voice of the enemy. Lord, I trust You to renew my strength as I sleep, filling me with Your presence and power for the new day. I surrender myself fully to Your care, knowing that I dwell in safety because of Your unfailing love. In Jesus' mighty name, Amen.

Prayer to Rebuke and Silence the Enemy

Scripture: "The Lord will cause your enemies who rise against you to be defeated before your face; they shall come out against you one way and flee before you seven ways." Deuteronomy 28:7

Prayer: Lord God, I thank You for the promise in Deuteronomy 28:7 that You will cause my enemies to be defeated before me. Today, I declare that every demonic spirit, attack, or plan of the enemy sent against me must flee in seven different directions. I rebuke the enemy and command silence to every voice of accusation, deception, and intimidation. Lord, let Your truth and light fill every area of my life, pushing back all darkness. I stand on Your Word, knowing that You fight for me and that no weapon formed against me can prosper. Father, I invite Your Holy Spirit to empower me, giving me boldness to resist the enemy and remain steadfast in faith. Thank You for being my defender and protector. I claim total victory in Jesus' name. Amen.

Prayer for Complete Deliverance and Victory

Scripture: "The Spirit of the Lord is on me, because He has anointed me to proclaim good news to the poor. He has sent me to proclaim freedom for the prisoners and recovery of sight for the blind, to set the oppressed free." (Luke 4:18)

Prayer: Lord Jesus, I thank You for coming to set the oppressed free, as stated in Luke 4:18. I stand in the fullness of Your deliverance tonight, declaring freedom from every demonic oppression, bondage, and attack over my life. By Your anointing, I proclaim liberty in every area of my life where the enemy has sought to enslave me. Father, I call upon the power of Your Spirit to break every chain, remove every shackle, and dismantle every stronghold that has been holding me back. I ask for complete restoration of my mind, body, and spirit. Lord, I surrender myself to Your Lordship, trusting that You have already won the victory on my behalf. Let Your power be made manifest in my life, and let every evidence of the enemy's work be erased. I declare that I am free, delivered, and walking in Your abundant life. In Jesus' mighty name, Amen.

Prayers Against Monitoring Spirits

Prayer of Deliverance

Scripture: "No weapon formed against you shall prosper, and every tongue which rises against you in judgment You shall condemn." Isaiah 54:17

Prayer: Heavenly Father, I declare that no weapon formed against me by monitoring spirits shall prosper. I silence every tongue and accusation in the spirit realm through the authority of Jesus Christ. I take authority over every demonic surveillance and declare that their plans are null and void. Let every plot and scheme against me be destroyed in Jesus' name. I thank You, Lord, for Your divine protection over my life, and I trust that You are my shield and refuge. I command every monitoring spirit to be bound, powerless, and rendered ineffective in the name of Jesus. No enemy can stand against Your power, and no curse or accusation shall take root in my life. Father, I ask that Your angels surround me and block every attempt of the enemy to infiltrate my thoughts, my emotions, or my life. I decree that I am hidden in Christ, and every assignment of the enemy shall be thwarted. I declare victory over every unseen force, knowing that You fight on my behalf. Thank You, Lord, for the authority You have given me in Christ. I claim my freedom and protection, and I walk in Your peace, knowing that I am covered by Your mighty hand. In Jesus' name, I pray. Amen.

Prayer for Divine Protection

Scripture: "For He shall give His angels charge over you, to keep you in all your ways." Psalm 91:11

Prayer: Lord, I call on Your angels to surround me and guard me against every spying eye and demonic surveillance. Protect me under Your wings and let no harm come near me. I trust in Your divine protection and Your promise that You are my refuge and fortress, my God in whom I trust. Father, I ask that Your angels stand as a mighty defense around me, blocking every attempt of the enemy to invade my thoughts, my life, or my peace. Let every spirit of surveillance be silenced and let every plan of the enemy be frustrated in the name of Jesus. Cover me with Your precious blood, Lord, and let no weapon formed against me prosper. I declare that I am hidden in Christ and secure in Your love. No evil can come near me because I am shielded by Your mighty power. Thank You, Lord, for Your constant protection. I walk in the peace of knowing that You are with me, guarding me from all harm. In Jesus' name, Amen.

Prayer to Cancel Assignments

Scripture: "Having disarmed principalities and powers, He made a public spectacle of them, triumphing over them in it." Colossians 2:15

Father, I cancel every assignment of monitoring spirits over my life. Through the victory of Christ on the cross, I declare their works null and void. Let them be disarmed and rendered powerless, in Jesus' name. Amen

Prayer to Blind Evil Watchers

Scripture: "Strike this army with blindness." 2 Kings 6:17-18

Prayer: Lord, just as You struck the enemy with blindness in Elisha's day, I ask You to blind every monitoring spirit assigned to my life. Let their sight be darkened, and their plans fail, in Jesus' name. Amen.

Prayer of Authority

Scripture: "Behold, I give you the authority to trample on serpents and scorpions, and over all the power of the enemy." Luke 10:19

Prayer: In the name of Jesus, I exercise the authority given to me. I trample on every demonic spirit watching and plotting against me. I declare their power broken, in Jesus' name. Amen.

Prayer for Freedom

Scripture: "Stand fast therefore in the liberty by which Christ has made us free." Galatians 5:1

Prayer: Lord, I stand firm in the freedom You have given me. I reject any form of spiritual bondage and declare myself free from every monitoring spirit. By Your power, I remain unshaken, in Jesus' name. Amen.

Prayer Against Familiar Spirits

Scripture: "Do not turn to mediums or familiar spirits; do not seek after them." Leviticus 19:31

Prayer: Father, I come before You with a heart of surrender, renouncing any connection to familiar spirits, whether knowingly or unknowingly. I break every tie, every stronghold, and every influence they have had over my life. In the mighty name of Jesus, I command them to leave now. They have no authority, no power, and no place in my life. I declare that I am set free by the power of Your Holy Spirit, and I am covered by the blood of Jesus. Thank You for Your protection, deliverance, and peace. In Jesus' name, Amen.

Prayer for Confusion

Scripture: "Let those be put to shame and brought to dishonor who seek after my life." Psalm 35:4

Prayer: Lord, let every monitoring spirit be confounded and confused. Scatter their plans and bring their works to nothing. I declare that every assignment of darkness is broken, and every strategy of the enemy is rendered powerless. In the mighty name of Jesus, I speak destruction over their schemes and declare that their efforts will bear no fruit. Lord, let shame and dishonor fall upon these spirits and all those who seek to do harm. I declare that they will be exposed, and their efforts thwarted. Your light will shine brightly, dispelling all darkness and revealing the truth. I trust that You, Lord, are fighting on my behalf, and that no weapon formed against me shall prosper. You are my defender, and Your power is greater than any force the enemy can send. Thank You for Your protection and victory. I stand firm in Your authority, knowing that You will bring all things to completion according to Your will. In Jesus' name, Amen.

Prayer for Heavenly Fire

Scripture: "For our God is a consuming fire." Hebrews 12:29

Prayer: Father, I ask You to release Your consuming fire to destroy every monitoring spirit that has been assigned to watch over me. Let Your fire burn every device they use and dismantle every altar they have set up against me. I declare that no weapon formed against me shall prosper, and I trust that You are my protector, shielding me from all evil. Let Your power bring complete destruction to every plan of the enemy, and let Your presence surround me with divine protection. In Jesus' name, Amen.

Prayer to Seal My Life

Scripture: "You were sealed with the Holy Spirit of promise." Ephesians 1:13

Prayer: Lord, I declare that my life is sealed by Your Holy Spirit. No evil eye or spirit can penetrate the covering of Your blood over my life. I am secure in You, and I trust that Your protection is constant and unbreakable. Your blood covers me completely, shielding me from every attack, every evil force, and every plan of the enemy. I proclaim that no weapon formed against me shall prosper, and no power of darkness shall have access to my life. I stand firm in the security of Your love and the assurance of Your victory over every demonic force. Thank You, Lord, for being my refuge and my fortress, for making me secure in Your presence. I walk in the peace that comes from knowing that You are my protector, and I trust that Your Holy

Spirit surrounds me with divine protection at all times. In Jesus' name, I pray. Amen.

Prayer to Break Evil Altars

Scripture: "Tear down the altar of Baal that your father has." Judges 6:25-26

Prayer: In Jesus' name, I tear down every evil altar empowering monitoring spirit against me. Let those altars be destroyed by the fire of the Holy Spirit. I declare that every demonic altar that has been raised against me is broken, dismantled, and completely nullified by the power of God. Lord, let Your consuming fire fall upon these altars and burn them to the ground. Let every spirit of monitoring and surveillance be rendered powerless, unable to function or carry out their plans. I command every legal ground the enemy has gained to be revoked, and I bind every demonic force operating from those altars in the name of Jesus. Father, I thank You for the victory You've already won for me on the cross. I claim that victory over every dark work, and I stand firm in the authority You've given me. I pray that Your fire will purify and protect, destroying every plot of the enemy and bringing me into a place of freedom and peace. In Jesus' name, I pray. Amen.

Prayer for Peace

Scripture: "And the peace of God will guard your hearts and minds through Christ Jesus." Philippians 4:7

Prayer: Lord, I thank You for Your perfect peace that surpasses all understanding. I ask that Your peace guard my heart and mind, keeping me free from fear of any monitoring spirit or demonic influence. I rest in the assurance of Your protection, knowing that You are my refuge and fortress. Surround me with Your divine presence and let nothing disturb the calm You provide. I place my trust in You, and I stand firm in Your peace, in Jesus' name. Amen.

Prayer Against Spiritual Spies

Scripture: Job 5:12 "He frustrates the devices of the crafty, so that their hands cannot carry out their plans."

Father, frustrate every plan of spiritual spies assigned to monitor me. Render their devices useless, in Jesus' name. I decree that their operations are paralyzed, their informants are confused, and their powers are rendered useless in Jesus' name. Father, I thank You that through Christ, I am victorious. My life is hidden in You, and no enemy can penetrate the divine covering over me. By faith, I walk boldly, free from fear, knowing that You have given me power to overcome every work of the enemy. In Jesus' mighty name, Amen.

Prayer to Break Generational Ties

Scripture: "Our fathers sinned and are no more, but we bear their iniquities." Lamentations 5:7

Prayer: Lord, I come before You, renouncing every generational tie that gives monitoring spirits legal access to my life. I break every connection and claim the freedom that is mine in Christ Jesus. As John 8:36 says, "If the Son sets you free, you will be free indeed." I declare that I am free from every spirit of surveillance and manipulation. Protect me with Your divine covering and let no weapon or spiritual force have power over me. I walk in the freedom and victory You have given me. In Jesus' name, Amen.

Prayer to Silence Evil Voices

Scripture: "Your voice shall be brought down to the ground." Isaiah 29:4

Prayer: Lord, silence every voice speaking against me in the spirit realm. Let their whispers and accusations be silenced, in Jesus' name. Amen. Heavenly Father, I thank You for Your divine protection over my life. I declare that no evil force shall monitor or speak over my destiny. I call upon Your mighty angels to surround me, shielding me from every demonic observer, every spiritual spy, and every monitoring spirit assigned against me.

By the power of the blood of Jesus, I dismantle every satanic mirror, crystal ball, spiritual drone, and demonic surveillance set up against me. Let their devices malfunction, and let confusion fall upon those who seek to track my progress. Just as You protected Daniel in the lion's den and Elisha from the armies of Syria, cover me with Your presence, Lord. Hide me under the shadow of Your wings, and let no harm come near me. In the mighty name of Jesus, I pray. Amen.

Prayer of Authority

Scripture: "Behold, I give you the authority to trample on serpents and scorpions, and over all the power of the enemy, and nothing shall by any means hurt you." Luke 10:19

Prayer: Lord Jesus, I thank You for giving me authority over all the power of the enemy. Right now, I stand on Your Word and exercise this divine authority against every monitoring spirit watching my life, my family, my ministry, and my destiny. I trample on every serpent and scorpion that has been assigned to track my movements and hinder my progress. I declare that their surveillance is destroyed by the fire of the Holy Spirit. Every demonic network set up to report my affairs back to the kingdom of darkness is dismantled now! Amen.

Prayer to Silence Evil Voices

Scripture: "Your voice shall be brought down to the ground; out of the dust your speech shall whisper." Isaiah 29:4

Heavenly Father, I come against every evil voice speaking against me in the spiritual realm. Whether they are whispering incantations, making evil decrees, or releasing negative words over my destiny, I declare them null and void in Jesus' name. Every demonic priest, occultist, witch, or sorcerer who has been assigned to monitor and manipulate my life—let their voices be silenced now! I command every evil declaration spoken over me to fall to the ground and bear no fruit. Let the blood of Jesus erase every curse, every word of failure, delay, and frustration spoken against me. I declare that only the voice of the Lord shall prevail in my life. His voice brings peace, prosperity, and protection. His words are life, and I align myself only with His promises. No monitoring spirit shall have dominion over my words, my prayers, or my destiny. In the name of Jesus Christ, I seal this prayer. Amen.

Prayer of Redemption

Scripture: "And they overcame him by the blood of the Lamb and by the word of their testimony, and they did not love their lives to the death." Revelation 12:11

Prayer: Mighty God, I stand upon the victory of the cross, where Jesus Christ shed His precious blood for my redemption. Through the power of the blood of the Lamb, I overcome every monitoring spirit that seeks to trap me in bondage, delay, and affliction. Father, I renounce every ancestral covenant, generational curse, or spiritual tie that may have granted access to these spirits in my life. Let the blood of Jesus speak for me where my name has been mentioned in demonic gatherings. Let every evil covenant be broken, every satanic contract be canceled, and every legal ground be removed in Jesus' name. Lord, I declare that I am redeemed, delivered, and set free. The blood of Jesus covers me from head to toe, shielding me from every demonic watcher. I am victorious by the blood, and my testimony shall be one of triumph, breakthrough, and divine favor. In Jesus' name, Amen.

Prayer Against Hidden Enemies

Scripture: "For nothing is secret that will not be revealed, nor anything hidden that will not be known and come to light." Luke 8:17

Prayer: Heavenly Father, I thank You for being the God who reveals secrets. You see all things, and no plan of the enemy is hidden from You. Today, I pray that every hidden enemy, every secret monitoring spirit, and every unseen force working against me be exposed and brought to judgment in Jesus' name. Lord, let Your light shine into every dark place. Expose those who pretend to be my friends but are secretly plotting my downfall. Reveal every hidden trap, every covert manipulation, and every demonic setup against me. Just as Haman's plot was exposed and turned against him, let every scheme of the enemy against me be reversed and destroyed. I decree and declare that I will walk in discernment. No enemy, whether spiritual or physical, shall operate undetected in my life. I declare that every adversary is unmasked and rendered powerless in Jesus' mighty name. Amen.

Prayer for a Hedge of Protection

Scripture: "Have You not made a hedge around him, around his household, and around all that he has on every side?" Job 1:10

Prayer: Father, just as You placed a hedge of protection around Job, I ask that You surround me, my family, my home, my finances, and my destiny with Your divine hedge. Let Your fire encircle me and prevent any monitoring spirit from gaining access to my life. I declare that no spiritual informant, no evil eye, no demonic agent shall penetrate the covering You have placed over me. Every arrow shot against me from afar shall be deflected. Every evil gaze directed at me shall be blinded. Every enchantment or divination sent my way shall be reversed. Lord,

I trust in Your protection. I will not fear, for You are my refuge and fortress. I rest in the assurance that no weapon formed against me shall prosper. In Jesus' mighty name, Amen.

Prayer of Victory

Scripture: "Yet in all these things we are more than conquerors through Him who loved us." Romans 8:37

Prayer: Lord Jesus, I thank You that I am more than a conqueror through You. No monitoring spirit, no satanic agent, and no demonic power can defeat me because I stand firm in Your victory. I declare that I am not a victim but a victor! Every chain of oppression is broken. Every door of affliction is shut. Every plot of darkness is dismantled. The enemy may try, but he will always fail, because I am covered by the blood of Jesus and sealed with the Holy Spirit. Today, I walk in total dominion. I decree that my destiny is secure, my blessings are protected, and my purpose is unstoppable. The plans of the enemy shall never prevail over my life. I rejoice in the assurance that I am victorious now and forever in Jesus' mighty name. Amen!

Prayers for Strength and Endurance

Prayer for Strength in the Battle

Scripture: "Finally, my brethren, be strong in the Lord and in the power of His might." Ephesians 6:10

Prayer: Heavenly Father, I acknowledge that my strength comes from You. In this spiritual battle, I will not rely on my own abilities but on Your mighty power. Strengthen my spirit, Lord, so I may not falter or grow weary. Help me to stand firm, clothed in Your armor, ready to resist every attack of the enemy. Let Your power fill me so that I can walk in victory. In Jesus' name, Amen.

Prayer for Renewed Strength

Scripture: "But those who wait on the Lord shall renew their strength; they shall mount up with wings like eagles, they shall run and not be weary, they shall walk and not faint." Isaiah 40:31

Prayer: Lord, I wait upon You because I know that in You, my strength is renewed. I refuse to let weariness and discouragement overtake me. Instead, I rise above my circumstances, mounting up with wings like eagles. Strengthen me to keep running the race of faith without growing weary. I receive fresh endurance to keep walking in Your will without fainting. Fill me with Your power, Lord, and let my soul be revived. In Jesus' name, Amen.

Prayer for Strength to Resist the Enemy

Scripture: "Therefore submit to God. Resist the devil and he will flee from you." James 4:7

Father, I submit myself fully to You. I take a stand against every scheme of the enemy that seeks to drain my strength and weaken my faith. Strengthen me, Lord, so that I will not give in to temptation, doubt, or fear. I resist the devil and every attack he sends my way. I declare that he must flee, for I am under Your divine covering. Keep me firm and steadfast, rooted in Your Word, in Jesus' name. Amen.

Prayer for Endurance Through Trials

Scripture: "We also glory in tribulations, knowing that tribulation produces perseverance; and perseverance, character; and character, hope." Romans 5:3-4

Lord, I thank You that even in the trials I face, You are working in me. Though the battle is intense, I will not be discouraged because I know You are producing perseverance in me. Strengthen me, Lord, to endure hardship and remain faithful. Build my character through every challenge, and let my hope remain anchored in You. I will not quit or give up, for I know that You are leading me to victory. In Jesus' name, Amen.

Prayer for Strength in Times of Fear

Scripture: "For God has not given us a spirit of fear, but of power and of love and of a sound mind." 2 Timothy 1:7

Lord, I reject every spirit of fear that tries to weaken me. You have given me a spirit of power, love, and a sound mind. Strengthen my heart, O God, that I may walk in boldness.

When the enemy tries to instill fear in me, remind me that I am victorious in You. Let my mind be at peace, and let my heart remain steadfast in faith. I declare that fear has no hold over me. In Jesus' name, Amen.

Prayer for Strength to Overcome Temptation

Scripture: "No temptation has overtaken you except such as is common to man; but God is faithful, who will not allow you to be tempted beyond what you are able, but with the temptation will also make the way of escape." 1 Corinthians 10:13

Prayer: Lord, I ask for strength to resist every temptation the enemy sets before me. When I feel weak, remind me that You always provide a way of escape. Strengthen my spirit to overcome sin and walk in purity. Let my heart be steadfast in righteousness and help me to choose Your ways over the desires of the flesh. I rely on Your power to keep me strong. In Jesus' name, Amen.

Prayer for Strength in Spiritual Warfare

Scripture: "For the weapons of our warfare are not carnal but mighty in God for pulling down strongholds." 2 Corinthians 10:4

Mighty God, I take up the weapons of spiritual warfare—the power of prayer, Your Word, and faith. Strengthen me to tear down every stronghold of the enemy. Let every demonic force that seeks to weaken me be destroyed. I declare that I am armed with Your truth and clothed in Your righteousness. No weapon formed against me shall prosper. In Jesus' name, Amen.

Prayer for Endurance in Faith

Scripture: Let us run with endurance the race that is set before us. Hebrews 12:1

Father, help me to run this race of faith with endurance. When I grow tired, refresh me. When I feel discouraged, lift me up. Strengthen my heart so that I may keep pressing forward. I refuse to give up, and I refuse to be distracted. Keep my focus on Jesus, my source of strength. In Jesus' name, Amen.

Prayer for Strength to Stand Firm

Scripture: "Watch, stand fast in the faith, be brave, be strong." 1 Corinthians 16:13

Prayer: Lord, I choose to stand fast in my faith. No matter what storms come against me, I will not be moved. Strengthen me to remain firm in my convictions and steadfast in my trust in You. Make me courageous and strong in the midst of battle. In Jesus' name, Amen.

Prayer for Strength Against Weariness

Scripture: "And let us not grow weary while doing good, for in due season we shall reap if we do not lose heart." Galatians 6:9

Father, when I feel weary and burdened, remind me of Your promises. Strengthen me to continue doing what is right, even when it seems difficult. I trust that my labor in You is not in vain, and in due season, I will reap a harvest. Help me to endure and not give up. In Jesus' name, Amen.

Prayer for Strength Through the Holy Spirit

Scripture: Not by might nor by power, but by My Spirit, says the Lord. Zechariah 4:6

Holy Spirit, fill me with Your power. I acknowledge that my own strength is not enough, but with You, I can overcome every obstacle. Strengthen me to walk in obedience and victory. In Jesus' name, Amen.

Prayer for Strength in Spiritual Battles

Scripture: For the Lord your God is He who goes with you, to fight for you against your enemies, to save you. Deuteronomy 20:4

Lord, I trust that You fight for me. I will not be afraid or discouraged, for You are with me. Strengthen me to stand my ground, knowing that victory belongs to You. In Jesus' name, Amen. Lord, strengthen me in every battle, help me endure in faith, keep me faithful in obedience, sustain me to finish my race, and empower me to live in victory. I trust in Your strength and Your power to sustain me all my days. In Jesus' mighty name, Amen! Pray these prayers with faith, knowing that God is your source of strength and endurance. He will empower you to overcome every spiritual battle.

Prayer for Strength to Wait on God

Scripture: Wait on the Lord; be of good courage, and He shall strengthen your heart; wait, I say, on the Lord! Psalm 27:14

Heavenly Father, waiting is not always easy, but I trust in Your perfect timing. When I feel anxious and impatient, remind me that You are working behind the scenes for my good. Strengthen my heart so that I do not grow weary in the waiting season. Let my faith remain steadfast, and help me to rest in Your promises, knowing that You will strengthen me as I wait. I choose to trust in You, Lord, and I know You will never fail me. In Jesus' name, Amen.

Prayer for Strength Against Discouragement

Scripture: "Have I not commanded you? Be strong and of good courage; do not be afraid, nor be dismayed, for the Lord your God is with you wherever you go." Joshua 1:9

Father, discouragement tries to weaken my heart and make me doubt Your promises. But I stand on Your Word, which tells me to be strong and courageous. I refuse to give in to fear, doubt, or despair because I know You are with me. Strengthen me in moments of weakness and remind me that You are my refuge. I will not be shaken because my hope is in You. In Jesus' name, Amen.

Prayer for Strength in Hard Times

Scripture: "God is our refuge and strength, a very present help in trouble." Psalm 46:1

Lord, in times of trouble, I run to You. You are my refuge and my source of strength. When life becomes overwhelming and I feel burdened, I know that You are my ever-present help. Strengthen my heart and sustain me through every challenge.

I lean on You, knowing that You will never leave nor forsake me. No matter what I face, I trust in Your power to carry me through. In Jesus' name, Amen.

Prayer for Strength to Keep Pressing Forward

Scripture: "I press toward the goal for the prize of the upward call of God in Christ Jesus." Philippians 3:14

Father, sometimes the journey feels long, and I feel tempted to give up. But I refuse to be discouraged. I choose to press on toward the goal You have set before me. Strengthen me to keep moving forward, even when I feel exhausted. Renew my determination, Lord, and remind me that there is a great reward awaiting me. I fix my eyes on You and will not be distracted by the trials of life. In Jesus' name, Amen.

Prayer for Strength to Walk in Obedience

Scripture: "Be strong and of good courage, do not fear nor be afraid of them; for the Lord your God, He is the One who goes with you. He will not leave you nor forsake you." Deuteronomy 31:6

Prayer: Lord, obeying You is not always easy, but I trust that Your way is always best. Give me the strength to follow Your commands, even when it is difficult. Help me to walk in faith and not in fear. I know that You are always with me, and You will never leave me alone in my obedience. Strengthen my resolve to walk in Your truth and live according to Your will. In Jesus' name, Amen.

Prayer for Endurance to Finish the Race

Scripture: "I have fought the good fight, I have finished the race, I have kept the faith." 2 Timothy 4:7

Lord, I do not want to start this journey strong but fail to finish well. Give me the endurance to keep going until I fulfill the purpose You have for me. When obstacles arise, strengthen my faith so that I may not stumble. Keep me focused on the eternal prize and give me the perseverance to complete the race You have set before me. I long to hear You say, 'Well done, good and faithful servant.' In Jesus' name, Amen.

Prayer for Strength to Overcome Every Attack

Scripture: "No weapon formed against you shall prosper, and every tongue which rises against you in judgment You shall condemn." Isaiah 54:17

Prayer: Mighty God, I know the enemy seeks to attack me, but I stand firm in Your promise that no weapon formed against me shall prosper. Strengthen me to withstand every assault on my faith, my mind, and my spirit. I take authority over every lie and scheme of the enemy, declaring that I am victorious in Christ. Fill me with Your power so that I may overcome every opposition. In Jesus' name, Amen.

Prayer for Strength to Live Victoriously

Scripture: "For whatever is born of God overcomes the world. And this is the victory that has overcome the world our faith." 1 John 5:4

Prayer: Father, I am born of You, and therefore, I am an overcomer. Strengthen me to live in the victory that Jesus has won for me. I refuse to live in defeat, discouragement, or fear. Fill me with faith, endurance, and courage so that I may walk in the fullness of Your promises. Let my life be a testimony of Your power and grace. In Jesus' name, Amen.

Prayers for Binding and Loosing

Note: These prayers incorporate binding and loosing based on Matthew 16:19 "I will give you the keys of the kingdom of heaven; whatever you bind on earth will be bound in heaven, and whatever you loose on earth will be loosed in heaven".

Binding the Spirit of Anger and Loosing Self-Control

Scripture: "He who is slow to anger is better than the mighty, and he who rules his spirit than he who takes a city." Proverbs 16:32

Prayer: Father, I come before You and bind every spirit of uncontrolled anger, rage, and wrath in my life. Your Word in James 1:19-20 teaches, "Be swift to hear, slow to speak, slow to wrath; for the wrath of man does not produce the righteousness of God." I refuse to let anger control me or cause harm to others. I loose self-control and patience over my emotions. Proverbs 16:32 says, "He who is slow to anger is better than the mighty, and he who rules his spirit than he who takes a city." Lord, give me a gentle spirit and a heart that responds with grace. Let my words and actions be guided by Your peace and wisdom. Help me to forgive quickly and not hold onto offense. Ephesians 4:26-27 reminds me, "Be angry, and do not sin: do not let the sun go down on your wrath, nor give place to the devil." I declare that I will walk in patience, love, and self-control, in Jesus' name, amen!

To bind every work of the enemy that is trying to hinder your purpose and destiny.

Scripture: "Truly I tell you, whatever you bind on earth will be bound in heaven, and whatever you loose on earth will be loosed in heaven." Matthew 18:18

Prayer: Father, I come before You in the name of Jesus, thanking You for the authority You've given me. I stand on Your Word, and I bind every work of the enemy that is set to hinder my progress and destiny. Your Word says in Matthew 18:18, "Whatever you bind on earth will be bound in heaven, and whatever you loose on earth will be loosed in heaven." Therefore, I bind every attack, scheme, and plan of the enemy that is coming against me, my family, and my purpose. I declare that every demonic force is bound in the name of Jesus. No weapon formed against me will prosper (Isaiah 54:17). I decree and declare that the enemy's plans are nullified by the power of the Holy Spirit. I claim victory over every attack, and I stand firm in Your promises. In Jesus' name, I pray. Amen.

Prayer for Loosing God's Will in Your Life

Scripture: "For I know the plans I have for you, declares the Lord, plans for welfare and not for evil, to give you a future and a hope." Jeremiah 29:11

Prayer: Heavenly Father, I thank You for the authority You have given me through Jesus Christ. In the mighty name of Jesus, I loose Your divine will over my life. I declare that Your purposes will come to pass in my life according to Jeremiah 29:11, which says, "For I know the plans I have for you, declares the Lord, plans for welfare and not for evil, to give you a future and a hope." I declare that every hindrance to Your plan is removed, and Your perfect will is being established in my life. I loose the blessings, favor, and provision You have in store for me. Thank You for guiding me into the future You've designed, filled with purpose and hope. In Jesus' name, Amen.

Prayer for Binding Strongholds

Scripture: "For the weapons of our warfare are not of the flesh but have divine power to destroy strongholds." 2 Corinthians 10:4

Prayer: Father, I thank You for Your power that is available to me. I bind every stronghold in my life that is preventing me from living fully in Your truth. Your Word says in 2 Corinthians 10:4, "For the weapons of our warfare are not of the flesh but have divine power to destroy strongholds." I declare that any stronghold of fear, doubt, addiction, or unbelief is bound in the name of Jesus. I demolish every argument and every pretension that sets itself up against the knowledge of God (2 Corinthians 10:5). I take captive every thought to make it obedient to Christ. I speak freedom, deliverance, and victory in every area of my life. In Jesus' name, Amen.

Prayer for Loosing Freedom and Deliverance

Scripture: "When Jesus saw her, he called her over and said, 'Woman, you are freed from your disability.'" Luke 13:12

Prayer: Lord, I thank You for the freedom You offer through Jesus Christ. I declare in the name of Jesus, according to Luke 13:12, "Woman, you are freed from your disability." I loose myself from every form of bondage, oppression, and affliction in Jesus' name. I declare that I am free from fear, sickness, poverty, and oppression, and I receive Your deliverance today. Just as You loosed the woman who was bent over in Luke 13:12, I declare that I am loosed from every burden and disability. I walk in Your freedom and victory, and I will not be bound any longer. In Jesus' name, Amen.

Prayer for Binding the Spirit of Rejection

Scripture: "For you did not receive the spirit of slavery to fall back into fear, but you have received the Spirit of adoption as sons, by whom we cry, 'Abba! Father!'" Romans 8:15

Prayer: Heavenly Father, I come before You and thank You for adopting me as Your child. I stand on Your Word in Romans 8:15, that I have not received the spirit of slavery or rejection, but the Spirit of adoption. I bind the spirit of rejection, fear, and insecurity in my life. I declare that I am accepted and loved by You, and that I do not need to fear. Lord, I release Your acceptance, love, and peace over my heart and mind. I receive Your perfect love, which casts out all fear (1 John 4:18). Thank You that I am Your child, and no spirit of rejection can have dominion over me. In Jesus' name, Amen.

Prayer for Binding Spirit of Poverty and Lack

Scripture: "And my God will supply every need of yours according to his riches in glory in Christ Jesus." Philippians 4:19

Prayer: Father, I thank You for being my Provider. Your Word says in Philippians 4:19, "And my God will supply every need of yours according to his riches in glory in Christ Jesus." In the name of Jesus, I bind the spirit of poverty, lack, and insufficiency that tries to operate in my life. I declare that I am not subject to the spirit of lack but to the abundance that comes from You. I release the spirit of provision, abundance, and prosperity over my finances, my home, and my family. I declare that You will provide for every need, and You will open doors of opportunity, favor, and increase. Thank You, Lord, that I am blessed and highly favored. In Jesus' name, Amen.

Prayer for Binding the Spirit of Confusion

Scripture: "For God is not a God of confusion but of peace. As in all the churches of the saints." 1 Corinthians 14:33

Prayer: Father, I thank You that You are a God of peace and not confusion. Your Word in 1 Corinthians 14:33 says, "For God is not a God of confusion but of peace." I bind the spirit of confusion, disorder, and unrest that tries to attack my mind, my relationships, and my decisions. I declare that I have the mind of Christ (1 Corinthians 2:16) and that I am led by Your peace and wisdom. I loose clarity, understanding, and divine direction into my life. May Your peace, which surpasses all understanding, guard my heart and mind in Christ Jesus (Philippians 4:7). In Jesus' name, Amen.

Prayer for Binding the Spirit of Fear

Scripture: "For God gave us a spirit not of fear but of power and love and self-control." 2 Timothy 1:7

Prayer: Father, I come before You in the name of Jesus, and I thank You that You have not given me a spirit of fear. According to 2 Timothy 1:7, "For God gave us a spirit not of fear but of power and love and self-control." I bind every spirit of fear, anxiety, and torment in my life, and I declare that it has no power over me. I release the spirit of power, love, and sound mind. I declare that I walk in boldness, confidence, and peace because You are with me. I will not be afraid, for You are my refuge and strength (Psalm 46:1). I trust in Your love and Your perfect plan for my life. In Jesus' name, Amen.

Prayers for Receiving Joy

Prayer for the Joy of the Lord as Strength

Scripture: "Do not grieve, for the joy of the Lord is your strength." Nehemiah 8:10

Prayer: Heavenly Father, I thank You that Your joy is my strength. The enemy seeks to steal my joy and replace it with fear, sadness, and discouragement, but I stand on Your promise that Your joy sustains me. I reject every spirit of heaviness and weariness, and I receive the supernatural joy that comes from Your presence. Lord, even when circumstances seem overwhelming, I choose to rejoice in You. I declare that the joy of the Lord will lift me above every trial and every attack of the enemy. Holy Spirit, fill me with overflowing joy that is not dependent on my situation but rooted in Your unchanging love. I rebuke every spirit of despair, depression, and anxiety, and I embrace the strength that Your joy brings. Thank You, Lord, for Your unshakable joy. In Jesus' name, Amen

Prayer for Overflowing Joy

Scripture: "You have made known to me the paths of life; You will fill me with joy in Your presence." Acts 2:28

Prayer: Father, I come before You seeking the fullness of joy that is found in Your presence. I know that true joy is not found in material things or temporary pleasures, but in You alone. Your Word says that in Your presence, there is fullness of joy, so I ask that You draw me closer to You. Fill my heart with joy that overflows, touching every area of my life. Remove every burden, every sorrow, and every worry that tries to weigh me down. Holy Spirit, I welcome You to pour out joy like a river within me, refreshing my soul and renewing my spirit. I will not be moved by circumstances, for my joy comes from the eternal, unshakable love of my Heavenly Father. Thank You, Lord, for filling me with a joy that never fades. In Jesus' name, Amen.

Prayer for Joy in the Midst of Trials

Scripture: "Consider it pure joy, my brothers and sisters, whenever you face trials of many kinds, because you know that the testing of your faith produces perseverance." James 1:2-3

Prayer: Lord, it is not always easy to find joy in difficult times, but Your Word commands me to consider it pure joy when I face trials. I choose to trust that You are working all things together for my good. I will not allow hardship to steal my joy, for I know that through every test, You are strengthening my faith. Lord, I surrender every struggle to You, and I ask for the supernatural joy that only comes from knowing You are in control. I declare that no trial, no hardship, and no attack of the enemy will rob me of the joy that is mine in Christ. I trust in Your perfect plan, and I rejoice in the victory that is already won. Thank You, Lord, for turning my trials into triumphs. In Jesus' name, Amen.

Prayer for Restoring Lost Joy

Scripture: "Restore to me the joy of Your salvation and grant me a willing spirit, to sustain me." Psalm 51:12

Prayer: Father, there have been times when I have lost my joy, when the weight of life has drained me of the happiness I once had in You. But today, I cry out for restoration. Restore to me the joy of Your salvation, O Lord. Let me remember the beauty of Your grace, the wonder of Your love, and the miracle of my redemption. I refuse to let the enemy steal the joy that comes from being Your child. Holy Spirit, revive my heart and refresh my soul. Let my joy be renewed as I set my eyes on You. Thank You for restoring my joy, Lord. In Jesus' name, Amen.

Prayer for Joy That Overcomes Anxiety

Scripture: "Rejoice in the Lord always. I will say it again: Rejoice! Do not be anxious about anything, but in every situation, by prayer and petition, with thanksgiving, present your requests to God." Philippians 4:4

Prayer: Father, I choose to rejoice in You always, even in the face of uncertainty. I reject every anxious thought and every worry that tries to rob me of my joy. Your Word commands me to rejoice and not to be anxious, so I lay every burden at Your feet. I choose faith over fear, peace over panic, and joy over sorrow. Lord, as I lift my prayers to You with thanksgiving, fill my heart with a peace that surpasses understanding. I trust in Your goodness, and I rejoice in Your unfailing love. Thank You for the joy that defeats every worry. In Jesus' name, Amen.

Prayer for Deliverance from the Spirit of Heaviness

Scripture: "The Spirit of the Lord... has anointed me... to give them the oil of joy instead of mourning, and a garment of praise instead of a spirit of despair." Isaiah 61:1

Prayer: Lord, I reject the spirit of heaviness that tries to weigh me down. You have anointed me to receive the oil of joy instead of mourning. I put on the garment of praise and cast off the cloak of despair. Every attack of discouragement, depression, and sorrow must flee in Jesus' name. I declare that I am filled with the joy of the Lord. My heart is light, my spirit is lifted, and my mouth is filled with praise. Thank You, Lord, for clothing me with joy. In Jesus' name, Amen.

Prayer for Joy in the Holy Spirit

Scripture: "For the kingdom of God is not a matter of eating and drinking, but of righteousness, peace and joy in the Holy Spirit." Romans 14:17

Prayer: Father, Your kingdom is a place of joy, and I ask that the Holy Spirit fill me with divine joy. Let me not seek joy in worldly things but in Your presence and power. Holy Spirit, overflow in my heart, saturate my soul, and bring me into a deeper experience of God's joy. I welcome Your presence to refresh me and renew my joy daily. Thank You for the joy that comes through Your Spirit. In Jesus' name, Amen.

Prayer for Joy in Worship

Scripture: "Shout for joy to the Lord, all the earth, worship the Lord with gladness." Psalm 100:1-2

Prayer: Lord, I worship You with gladness! I lift my voice in praise and thanksgiving, for You are worthy of all my joy. As I worship, let every burden be lifted and every chain be broken. I rejoice in Your presence, and I declare that no circumstance will steal my song. Thank You for the joy that fills my soul as I worship You. In Jesus' name, Amen.

Prayer for Joy in Victory Over the Enemy

Scripture: "But let all who take refuge in You be glad; let them ever sing for joy." Psalm 5:11

Prayer: Lord, I take refuge in You, and I rejoice in the victory that is mine in Christ. Every plan of the enemy against my joy is defeated. I stand victorious, singing with joy because You are my defender, my shield, and my deliverer. Thank You for the joy of victory! In Jesus' name, Amen.

Prayer for a Life Filled with Joy

Scripture: "May the God of hope fill you with all joy and peace as you trust in Him." Romans 15:13

Prayer: Lord, I ask that You fill me with joy and peace as I place my trust in You. Let my life be marked by overflowing joy that draws others to You. I choose to live in the fullness of joy that only You provide. Thank You, Lord, for making my life a testimony of Your joy. In Jesus' name, Amen.

Prayer for Joy in God's Presence

Scripture: "You make known to me the path of life; in Your presence there is fullness of joy; at Your right hand are pleasures forevermore." Psalm 16:11

Prayer: Father, I come before You, thanking You for the promise that in Your presence there is fullness of joy (Psalm 16:11). I desire to walk in Your presence every day, to experience the deep, overflowing joy that comes from knowing You. I rebuke the enemy's attempts to distract me, to pull my focus away from Your goodness. Lord, fill me with Your joy, which cannot be shaken by circumstances or situations. Let Your joy become the foundation of my life, grounding me in peace, hope, and unwavering faith. I choose to draw near to You, knowing that as I seek Your face, You will fill me with joy that overflows. Thank You for Your constant presence, where my soul finds rest and joy. In Jesus' name, Amen.

Prayer for the Joy of Salvation

Scripture: "Restore to me the joy of Your salvation and grant me a willing spirit, to sustain me." Psalm 51:12

Prayer: Lord, I come before You asking for a restoration of the joy of my salvation (Psalm 51:12). I recognize that at times, I have become distracted by the trials of life and have allowed my joy to fade. But Your Word says that the joy of salvation is a gift, and I desire that joy to fill me again. Father, revive my spirit with the gladness that comes from knowing I am saved, forgiven, and secure in Your love. Let my heart overflow with gratitude and joy for the work You have done in my life. I thank You for the sacrifice of Jesus and for the freedom that

His blood has brought me. May this joy continue to sustain me and lead me forward in faith. In Jesus' name, Amen.

Prayer for Joy in the Holy Spirit

Scripture: "For the kingdom of God is not a matter of eating and drinking, but of righteousness, peace and joy in the Holy Spirit." Romans 14:17

Prayer: Holy Spirit, I thank You for the joy You bring into my life. Your joy is not based on what I have or don't have, but on the righteousness and peace that come from being in right relationship with God. I surrender my heart to You today and ask You to fill me with the joy that transcends understanding. I refuse to be weighed down by the cares of this world. Holy Spirit, infuse me with the peace and joy that come from living in Your presence. I choose to rejoice in You, knowing that my joy is rooted in my salvation and the eternal life I have in Christ. Let Your joy overflow in my life, and may it be a testimony to all who encounter me. In Jesus' name, Amen.

Prayer for Joy in Times of Loss

Scripture: "Weeping may endure for a night, but joy comes in the morning." Psalm 30:5

Prayer: Father, I come to You with a heavy heart, acknowledging my grief and sorrow. But I thank You that Your Word promises that joy comes in the morning (Psalm 30:5). I trust in Your faithfulness, and I believe that no matter the pain I feel, You are working to bring me joy once again. Lord, I lay my burdens before You and ask You to replace my sorrow with the joy of Your healing. I stand on the promise that even in the darkest moments, You will turn my mourning into dancing. Holy Spirit, comfort me in my sorrow, and fill my heart with the hope and joy that only You can provide. Thank You, Lord, for the joy that will rise within me. In Jesus' name, Amen.

Prayer for Joy in Overcoming Fear

Scripture: "The joy of the Lord is your strength." Nehemiah 8:10

Prayer: Lord, I thank You for the strength that Your joy gives me (Nehemiah 8:10). Fear has tried to creep into my life, stealing my peace and joy, but I stand firm in Your Word. I declare that Your joy will be my strength, and fear has no place in my heart. I refuse to be intimidated by the enemy's lies or by the circumstances that try to overwhelm me. Instead, I choose to rejoice in You, knowing that Your joy will give me the courage to face any challenge. I pray for a deep, unshakable joy that remains steadfast regardless of the storm. Thank You, Lord, for empowering me with Your strength and joy, which are greater than any fear. In Jesus' name, Amen.

Prayer for Joy in the Knowledge of God's Goodness

Scripture: "Taste and see that the Lord is good; blessed is the one who takes refuge in Him." Psalm 34:8

Prayer: Father, I thank You for Your unfailing goodness (Psalm 34:8). I choose today to focus on Your goodness and to rejoice in Your blessings. Your Word tells me to taste and see that You are good, and I can testify to that truth from my own life. You have been faithful in every season, and I trust in Your continual goodness. I choose to rejoice in who You are and all that You have done for me. Thank You for the joy that comes from knowing You and seeing Your goodness in every part of my life. Lord, continue to show me Your goodness and fill my heart with the joy that only You can provide. In Jesus' name, Amen.

Prayer for Joy in Victory Over the Enem

Scripture: "But let all who take refuge in You be glad; let them ever sing for joy. Spread Your protection over them, that those who love Your name may rejoice in You." Psalm 5:11

Prayer: Lord, I thank You for the victory that You have already won over the enemy. You are my refuge and my fortress, and I find joy in the protection You provide. I know that no weapon formed against me will prosper, and I stand firm in Your victory over sin, death, and darkness. Father, I declare that the enemy has no authority in my life. I will not allow fear, doubt, or anxiety to steal my joy. Instead, I choose to rejoice in the victory I have in Christ. Holy Spirit, protect me, surround me with Your peace, and fill my heart with joy as I walk in the victory that You have given me. In Jesus' name, Amen.

Prayer for Joy in the Knowledge of God's Faithfulness

Scripture: "Great is His faithfulness; His mercies begin afresh each morning." Lamentations 3:23

Prayer: Father, I thank You for Your unwavering faithfulness (Lamentations 3:23). Your Word reminds me that Your mercies are new every morning, and I rejoice in that truth. When I look back on my life, I can see how You have been faithful in every season. Lord, even when I could not see the way, You have been with me every step of the journey. I thank You for the joy that comes from knowing You are always with me, never failing, never leaving. Today, I rest in Your faithfulness and choose to let that truth fill me with unshakeable joy. Thank You, Lord, for Your never-ending love and faithfulness. In Jesus' name, Amen.

Prayer for Joy in the Restoration of My Soul

Scripture: "He restores my soul. He leads me in paths of righteousness for His name's sake." Psalm 23

Prayer: Father, I thank You for Your restorative power in my life (Psalm 23:3). You are the God who restores, heals, and renews. Today, I bring before You any brokenness, weariness, or pain, asking You to restore my soul. I choose to trust in Your ability to heal me and make me whole. Father, lead me in the paths of righteousness and fill me with the joy that comes from walking with You. I thank You for Your promises of restoration and for the joy that accompanies Your work in my life. I will rejoice in Your goodness and trust that You will continue to guide me on the path of life. In Jesus' name, Amen

Prayer for Joy in Overflowing Abundance

Scripture: "The Lord will make you abound in prosperity, in the fruit of your womb, and in the fruit of your livestock, and in the fruit of your ground, within the land that the Lord swore to your fathers to give you." Deuteronomy 28:11

Prayer: Lord, I thank You for the abundant blessings You have poured out in my life (Deuteronomy 28:11). Your Word promises that You will make me abound in prosperity, and I rejoice in that truth. I refuse to let lack, scarcity, or worry rob me of my joy. I choose to celebrate the blessings You have given me—both big and small. Lord, let Your joy overflow in my life as I recognize the abundance of Your goodness. I pray that Your joy would be a testimony of Your faithfulness and provision. Thank You, Lord, for blessing me abundantly and for filling my heart with joy. In Jesus' name, Amen.

Prayers to Bless and Protect Your Home

Prayer for God's Protection Over Your Home

Scripture: "The Lord will watch over your coming and going both now and forevermore." Psalm 121:8

Prayer: Heavenly Father, I thank You for the promise that You watch over our every step, and You are a constant protector over our home. Your Word says that You will watch over our coming and going both now and forevermore (Psalm 121:8). Lord, I ask for Your divine protection to surround my home. Protect us from any harm, danger, or evil that may seek to come against us. Cover our home with Your angels, and let no weapon formed against us prosper. I place this household under Your protection and declare that we are safe in Your care. Keep us from all harm and bless our dwelling with Your peace. In Jesus' name, Amen.

Prayer for God's Presence to Dwell in Your Home

Scripture: "And let the peace of Christ rule in your hearts, to which indeed you were called in one body. And be thankful." Colossians 3:15

Prayer: Father God, I invite Your presence into every room of our home. I ask that the peace of Christ would rule in our hearts and fill every space with His calming presence (Colossians 3:15). May Your peace reign in our home, keeping strife, division, and negativity far from us. Let Your love flow through our interactions and relationships, bringing unity and harmony. I pray that as we dwell in this home, we would constantly be reminded of Your goodness and faithfulness. Thank You for being with us and guiding us every day. In Jesus' name, Amen.

Prayer for Protection from Evil Spirits

Scripture: "For He will command His angels concerning you to guard you in all your ways." Psalm 91:11

Prayer: Lord, I stand on Your promise that You will command Your angels to guard us in all our ways (Psalm 91:11). I ask You to send Your mighty angels to stand guard over our home and protect us from any evil spirits, curses, or dark forces that may try to enter. I plead the blood of Jesus over every entryway and every room in this home. Let no evil spirit have a place in this dwelling. I declare that this home is consecrated and dedicated to You, Lord. Fill every corner with Your holy presence and keep us safe from the enemy's schemes. In Jesus' name, Amen.

Prayer for Financial Blessings and Provision in Your Home

Scripture: "And my God will supply every need of yours according to His riches in glory in Christ Jesus." Philippians 4:19

Prayer: Father, I thank You for Your faithfulness in providing for all our needs (Philippians 4:19). I ask that You bless this home with financial provision and abundance. May there be no lack, and may You open the doors of blessing for us. We trust You to provide for every need—whether it be for food, shelter, clothing, or any other necessity. Lord, I pray that this home would be a place where we continually experience Your provision and give You glory for Your abundant goodness. May we be good stewards of what You provide and use it to bless others. In Jesus' name, Amen.

Prayer for Peace and Harmony in Your Home

Scripture: "And the peace of God, which surpasses all understanding, will guard your hearts and your minds in Christ Jesus." Philippians 4:7

Prayer: Lord, I ask for Your peace to fill our home and guard our hearts and minds (Philippians 4:7). Let Your peace surpasses all understanding and bring an atmosphere of calm and rest to this house. Where there has been tension, I pray for reconciliation. Where there has been unrest, I pray for Your perfect peace to settle in. Let our words, actions, and thoughts be filled with Your peace, and may this home be a place where love and understanding abound. I rebuke all spirits of anxiety, fear, and discord, and I ask You to replace them with the peace of Christ. In Jesus' name, Amen.

Prayer to Consecrate Your Home to God

Scripture: "As for me and my house, we will serve the Lord." Joshua 24:15

Prayer: Heavenly Father, today I consecrate this home to You. As for me and my house, we choose to serve the Lord (Joshua 24:15). We commit every room, every corner, and every person who enters this place to You. We invite You to take full control of our lives and our home. May every activity that takes place here be pleasing to You. Let this home be a place of worship, prayer, and fellowship. I dedicate it as a sanctuary for Your presence, a place where Your will is done, and Your name is glorified. In Jesus' name, Amen.

Prayer for Protection from Destruction and Calamity

Scripture: "No weapon formed against you shall prosper, and every tongue which rises against you in judgment you shall condemn." Isaiah 54:17

Prayer: Lord, I stand on Your promise that no weapon formed against us shall prosper (Isaiah 54:17). I declare that this home is shielded from all forms of destruction, calamity, and harm. Protect us from natural disasters, accidents, and any unforeseen danger. I ask that You would place a hedge of protection around our family, and that no weapon—whether physical or spiritual—will be able to harm us. We trust in Your divine protection and claim victory over any attacks that may come against this home. We are safe in Your hands, Lord. In Jesus' name, Amen.

Prayer for Spiritual Growth and Blessing in Your Home

Scripture: "But the fruit of the Spirit is love, joy, peace, forbearance, kindness, goodness, faithfulness, gentleness and self-control." Galatians 5:22-23

Prayer: Father, I pray that this home would be a place where the fruit of the Spirit thrives (Galatians 5:22-23). Let love, joy, peace, and kindness abound in our relationships with one another. I pray for a spirit of unity, understanding, and respect to flow through this household. May we encourage each other in faith and build one another up in love. Let Your Holy Spirit dwell richly among us, teaching us to be more like Christ in our thoughts, actions, and attitudes. May our home be filled with spiritual growth and be a beacon of Your light to others. In Jesus' name, Amen.

Prayer for Rest and Refreshment in Your Home

Scripture: "Come to Me, all you who are weary and burdened, and I will give you rest." Matthew 11:28

Prayer: Lord, I ask that You would grant rest and refreshment to all who dwell in this home (Matthew 11:28). In this busy world, it is easy to become weary, but You promise to give rest to those who come to You. I pray that this home would be a sanctuary of rest where we can lay down our burdens and find renewal in Your presence. Fill this home with peace and tranquility, where everyone who enters can feel Your comfort. Let Your presence be the rest that revives us. Thank You for Your promise to sustain and refresh us. In Jesus' name, Amen.

Prayer for Blessing and Provision for Your Household

Scripture: "Blessed shall you be when you come in, and blessed shall you be when you go out." Deuteronomy 28:6

Prayer: Father, I ask for Your blessings to be upon our home, both now and forever. Your Word promises that we will be blessed when we come in and when we go out (Deuteronomy 28:6). I claim this blessing over our household today. May Your favor rest upon each person who lives here, and may we experience Your provision and protection in every area of our lives. I pray that Your blessing would flow into every part of our home from our finances to our relationships to our health. Thank You, Lord, for Your abundant blessings that overflow into our lives. We give You all the glory and praise. In Jesus' name, Amen.

Prayers to Bless and Protect Your Children

Prayer for Protection from Evil and Harm

Scripture: "The angel of the Lord encamps around those who fear Him and delivers them." Psalm 34:7

Prayer: Father, I thank You for the promise that Your angels are encamped around those who fear You and that You deliver them from all harm (Psalm 34:7). I ask for Your divine protection over my children. Guard them from all evil, physical harm, and spiritual attack. I declare that no weapon formed against them will prosper, and that Your angels will stand watch over them, guiding them and protecting them wherever they go. Surround them with Your heavenly protection and shield them from the enemy's schemes. I trust in Your faithful care over their lives, Lord. In Jesus' name, Amen.

Prayer for Wisdom and Guidance for Your Children

Scripture: "If any of you lacks wisdom, let him ask of God, who gives to all liberally and without reproach, and it will be given to him." James 1:5

Prayer: Father, I pray for Your wisdom to guide my children in every decision they make (James 1:5). Lord, as they grow, grant them discernment, understanding, and insight. Help them to make choices that honor You and lead them to a life of purpose and fulfillment. Protect their hearts and minds from confusion and lies and help them to discern Your voice above all others.

I ask that You guide them through every challenge and opportunity, filling them with a spirit of wisdom and understanding. In Jesus' name, Amen.

Prayer for Strength and Courage for Your Children

Scripture: "Be strong and courageous. Do not be afraid or terrified because of them, for the Lord your God goes with you; He will never leave you nor forsake you." Deuteronomy 31:6

Prayer: Lord, I pray for strength and courage for my children as they face the challenges of life (Deuteronomy 31:6). May they never be afraid or discouraged, for You are always with them. I ask You to instill within them a bold spirit, knowing that You are their protector and that You will never leave them. When fear tries to take hold, may they stand strong in Your promises. Let them know that they can face anything because You are with them, guiding them every step of the way. In Jesus' name, Amen.

Prayer for Their Salvation and Relationship with God

Scripture: "Train up a child in the way he should go; even when he is old he will not depart from it." Proverbs 22:6

Prayer: Lord, I pray for the salvation of my children, that they would come to know You personally and develop a deep, intimate relationship with You. Your Word promises that when we train up a child in the way they should go, they will not depart from it (Proverbs 22:6). I claim this promise over my children. I pray that Your Holy Spirit would draw them near to You, open their hearts to Your love, and lead them to salvation in Jesus Christ. May they grow up to be strong men and women of faith, firmly rooted in Your truth. In Jesus' name, Amen.

Prayer for Protection from ive Influences

Scripture: "Do not be deceived: 'Bad company ruins good morals.'" 1 Corinthians 15:33

Prayer: Father, I pray that You would protect my children from negative influences and harmful relationships (1 Corinthians 15:33). Shield them from the wrong friends, teachers, or environments that could lead them away from Your path. Surround them with godly influences and people who will encourage their faith, uplift them, and guide them to truth. I ask that You help them to recognize harmful influences and give them the strength to stand firm in their beliefs. Let them be a light in the darkness, drawing others toward You. In Jesus' name, Amen.

Prayer for Health and Healing for Your Children

Scripture: "But He was pierced for our transgressions; He was crushed for our iniquities; upon Him was the chastisement that brought us peace, and with His wounds we are healed." (Isaiah 53:5)

Prayer: Lord, I ask for Your healing touch upon my children. Your Word says that by the wounds of Jesus, we are healed (Isaiah 53:5), and I claim this promise for their health. I pray that You would protect their bodies from illness, injury, and disease. If any sickness or affliction is present, I ask that You heal them completely. Restore their strength and energy and let them grow in health and vitality. I trust in Your power to heal and protect their physical bodies. In Jesus' name, Amen.

Prayer for Emotional and Mental Well-Being

Scripture: "Do not be anxious about anything, but in everything by prayer and supplication with thanksgiving let your requests be made known to God. And the peace of God, which surpasses all understanding, will guard your hearts and your minds in Christ Jesus." Philippians 4:6-7

Prayer: Father, I lift my children's emotional and mental well-being to You. Your Word tells us not to be anxious, but to bring everything before You with thanksgiving, and Your peace will guard our hearts and minds (Philippians 4:6-7). I pray that Your peace would guard my children's hearts, helping them to overcome anxiety, fear, and worry. Fill them with Your calming presence and give them the emotional resilience to face life's struggles. May they know that they are loved, and may they always turn to You for comfort and strength in times of difficulty. In Jesus' name, Amen.

Prayer for Their Future and Purpose

Scripture: "For I know the plans I have for you, declares the Lord, plans for welfare and not for evil, to give you a future and a hope." Jeremiah 29:11

Prayer: Lord, I thank You for the plans You have for my children's future. Your Word says that You have plans for them—plans to prosper them and give them a hope and a future (Jeremiah 29:11). I pray that You would reveal Your purpose for their lives, and that they would walk in the destiny You have prepared for them. Help them to discover their gifts and talents and to use them for Your glory. May they always seek Your will and trust in Your guidance as they move forward into their future. In Jesus' name, Amen.

Prayer for Strength to Resist Temptation

Scripture: "No temptation has overtaken you that is not common to man. God is faithful, and He will not let you be tempted beyond your ability, but with the temptation, He will also provide the way of escape, that you may be able to endure it." 1 Corinthians 10:13

Prayer: Father, I pray for strength for my children to resist temptation and stand firm in their faith (1 Corinthians 10:13). I know that You are faithful, and You promise that You will always provide a way of escape from temptation. I pray that You would help them to recognize temptation when it comes and to choose the path of righteousness. Give them the strength and wisdom to flee from anything that would lead them away from You. I trust that You will be their refuge and help in times of trial. In Jesus' name, Amen.

Prayer for Blessing and Prosperity for Your Children

Scripture: "Blessed shall you be when you come in, and blessed shall you be when you go out." Deuteronomy 28:6

Prayer: Lord, I pray that Your blessings would rest upon my children as they go about their day (Deuteronomy 28:6). Bless them when they come in and when they go out. I ask that You would bless their studies, their friendships, their health, and all their endeavors. May Your favor and provision follow them all the days of their lives. I pray that they would live lives that bring You glory, and that they would be a blessing to everyone around them. Thank You, Lord, for Your abundant blessings over my children. In Jesus' name, Amen.

Prayer for Spiritual Shield and Protection for Your Children

Scripture: "But the Lord is faithful. He will strengthen you and guard you from the evil one." 2 Thessalonians 3

Prayer: Heavenly Father, I thank You for Your faithfulness and Your promises that You will strengthen and guard my children from the evil one (2 Thessalonians 3:3). I ask You to build a spiritual shield of protection around them, surrounding them with Your divine armor. Protect their hearts and minds from the attacks of the enemy, from every temptation, and from all forms of evil. May Your Holy Spirit guard them against negativity, fear, and lies. Help them to grow in strength and courage, knowing that You are always by their side. Let them walk in the fullness of Your peace and power, standing firm in their identity in Christ. Thank You, Lord, for guarding their steps and being their ever-present help. In Jesus' name, Amen.

Prayer for Boldness and Courage to Stand for Christ

Scripture: "For God gave us a spirit not of fear but of power and love and self-control." 2 Timothy 1:7

Prayer: Lord God, I ask that You fill my children with the spirit of power, love, and self-control, as Your Word promises

(2 Timothy 1:7). Remove all fear and insecurity and replace it with boldness and courage to stand for You in every area of their lives. May they never be ashamed of the gospel but boldly declare Your truth, no matter the pressure from the world. Help them to be lights in darkness, speaking words of truth and love. Strengthen them to resist peer pressure, to walk according to Your Word, and to boldly represent Christ wherever they go. I pray they will shine brightly in their schools, friendships, and communities. In Jesus' name, Amen.

Prayer for Protection from Harmful Environments

Scripture: "The name of the Lord is a strong tower; the righteous run to it and are safe." Proverbs 18:10

Prayer: Father, I thank You that You are our strong tower and refuge (Proverbs 18:10). I ask You to protect my children from harmful environments, toxic relationships, and any places where their hearts and minds could be led astray. Surround them with Your presence and keep them safe in Your refuge. I pray that they would always run to You for safety when they face challenges or difficult situations. Let them discern when something is not of You and give them the courage to step away. I also ask that You place godly influences in their lives to help them grow in faith. Thank You for being their protector and guide. In Jesus' name, Amen.

Prayer for Emotional Healing and Strength

Scripture: "He heals the brokenhearted and binds up their wounds." Psalm 147

Prayer: Lord, I pray for emotional healing and strength for my children. Your Word says that You heal the brokenhearted and bind up their wounds (Psalm 147:3). I ask You to heal any emotional wounds that they may carry whether from past hurt, rejection, or trauma. I pray for Your peace to soothe their hearts and for Your strength to rise within them. Teach them how to process their emotions in a healthy way and surround them with love and support. I pray that Your healing touch would bring restoration to their minds, and that they would grow in emotional resilience and wisdom. May they always feel Your presence near, comforting them in times of difficulty. In Jesus' name, Amen.

Prayer for Provision and Prosperity in Their Lives

Scripture: "And my God will supply every need of yours according to His riches in glory in Christ Jesus." Philippians 4:19

Prayer: Father, I pray for Your provision and prosperity to flow into every area of my children's lives. Your Word promises that You will supply all of our needs according to Your riches in glory in Christ Jesus (Philippians 4:19). I ask You to bless them with everything they need to succeed, whether in their education, relationships, or future endeavors. Open doors of opportunity for them and provide for them in abundance. I pray that they would experience Your faithfulness in every area of their lives and trust that You will always provide for them. May they never lack, but instead, live in Your fullness and abundance. Thank You for Your generous provision and for being their ultimate provider. In Jesus' name, Amen.

Prayers to Praise and Give Thanks to God

Prayer of Thanksgiving for God's Goodness

Scripture: "Oh give thanks to the Lord, for He is good; for His steadfast love endures forever!" 1 Chronicles 16:34

Prayer: Heavenly Father, I come before You with a heart full of gratitude. You are so good, and Your steadfast love endures forever (1 Chronicles 16:34). Thank You for Your kindness, Your mercy, and the countless blessings You pour into my life every day. You have been faithful in every season, and I praise You for Your constant presence and provision. I give You thanks for Your goodness, for Your love that never fails, and for Your faithfulness that never wavers. May my life be a continual offering of praise to You, the God who is always good. In Jesus' name, Amen.

Prayer of Praise for God's Holiness

Scripture: "Holy, holy, holy is the Lord of hosts; the whole earth is full of His glory!" Isaiah 6: 3

Prayer: Lord God Almighty, I praise You for Your holiness. You are holy, holy, holy, and the whole earth is filled with Your glory (Isaiah 6:3). I stand in awe of Your purity, Your righteousness, and Your perfect nature. You are the Creator of the universe, yet You are near to each of us, loving us with an unfathomable love. I worship You, for You are set apart, incomparable, and glorious. May my life reflect Your holiness and bring honor to Your name. I give You praise for who You are, and I thank You for inviting me to stand in Your presence. In Jesus' name, Amen.

Prayer of Praise for God's Protection

Scripture: "The Lord is my rock, my fortress, and my deliverer; my God, my rock, in whom I take refuge." Psalm 18:2

Prayer: Lord, I praise You as my rock, my fortress, and my deliverer (Psalm 18:2). You have protected me from countless dangers, and Your hand of safety has been upon me and my family. Thank You for being our refuge, for sheltering us from the storms of life. When I feel weak, You are my strength; when I face battles, You are my shield. I give You all the glory for Your protection and for the peace You provide in every circumstance. I trust in Your stronghold and place my confidence in You, knowing that You will always deliver me. In Jesus' name, Amen.

Prayer of Thanks for God's Provision

Scripture: "And my God will supply every need of yours according to His riches in glory in Christ Jesus." Philippians 4:19

Prayer: Father, I thank You for Your abundant provision. Your Word promises that You will supply every need of mine according to Your riches in glory in Christ Jesus (Philippians 4:19). You have faithfully provided for my family and me in ways I cannot even count. Thank You for meeting our physical, emotional, and spiritual needs. You are our provider, and I trust

You completely. I give You praise for Your generosity and for making a way even when I couldn't see one. I am grateful for Your abundant blessings, and I will continue to trust in Your perfect provision. In Jesus' name, Amen.

Prayer of Praise for God's Faithfulness

Scripture: "The Lord is faithful to all His promises and loving toward all He has made." Psalm 145:13

Prayer: Lord, I praise You for Your unwavering faithfulness. Your Word declares that You are faithful to all Your promises and loving toward all You have made (Psalm 145:13). I thank You for the promises You've kept in my life, for Your unfailing love, and for Your constant presence. Even in the midst of challenges, I can always trust in Your faithfulness. You have never left me, and You will never forsake me. I give You praise for being a God of integrity and reliability. I trust that Your promises will continue to unfold in my life. In Jesus' name, Amen.

Prayer of Praise for God's Love

Scripture: "For the mountains may depart and the hills be removed, but my steadfast love shall not depart from you, and my covenant of peace shall not be removed," says the Lord, who has compassion on you. Isaiah 54:10

Prayer: Father, I thank You for Your everlasting love. Your love is steadfast, unshakable, and unconditional. You have promised that even if the mountains depart and the hills are removed, Your love for me will not depart (Isaiah 54:10). I praise You for a love that never fails, a love that covers all my sins and shortcomings. I am humbled by the depth of Your compassion and grace. May my heart always reflect the love You've poured out for me. Thank You for loving me with an everlasting love. In Jesus' name, Amen.

Prayer of Thanks for God's Healing Power

Scripture: "He heals the brokenhearted and binds up their wounds." Psalm 147

Prayer: Lord, I give You thanks for Your healing power. Your Word tells me that You heal the brokenhearted and bind up their wounds (Psalm 147:3). I praise You for being the great Physician who heals not only physical ailments but also emotional and spiritual wounds. Thank You for mending the broken pieces of my life and for restoring me when I have been hurting. I trust in Your healing touch and rejoice in the freedom You bring. I give You praise for Your tender care and for the restoration You bring to my body, mind, and spirit. In Jesus' name, Amen.

Prayer of Praise for God's Mercy

Scripture: "But the mercy of the Lord is from everlasting to everlasting on those who fear Him, and His righteousness to children's children." Psalm 103:17

Prayer: Heavenly Father, I praise You for Your mercy, which is from everlasting to everlasting (Psalm 103:17). Thank You for showing me mercy when I didn't deserve it, for forgiving my sins, and for extending grace to me every day. Your mercy is new every morning, and I am forever grateful for Your compassion and forgiveness. I worship You for Your kindness and for the way You continually show mercy to those who fear You. Thank You for your unending love and grace. I give You praise for Your mercy that covers all my transgressions. In Jesus' name, Amen.

Prayer of Thanksgiving for God's Sovereignty

Scripture: "Our God is in the heavens; He does all that He pleases." Psalm 115:3

Prayer: Lord, I praise You for Your sovereignty. You are in the heavens, and You do all that You please (Psalm 115:3). I thank You for being in control of everything in my life, for Your perfect will being accomplished in every situation. Even when I don't understand the trials I face, I trust that You are sovereign overall. Your plan is higher than mine, and Your timing is perfect. I give You thanks for knowing what is best for me and for guiding my steps according to Your will. I praise You for being the King over all creation and for Your authority in every detail of my life. In Jesus' name, Amen.

Prayer of Praise for God's Eternal Nature

Scripture: "Before the mountains were brought forth, or ever You had formed the earth and the world, from everlasting to everlasting You are God." Psalm 90:2

Prayer: Lord, I praise You for Your eternal nature. From everlasting to everlasting, You are God (Psalm 90:2). You have no beginning and no end, and Your reign is eternal. I worship

You as the Alpha and the Omega, the Creator of time and all that exists. Thank You for being unchanging and eternal, a firm foundation in a world that is always shifting. I give You all the praise for being the eternal God who holds everything in His hands. May I always find peace in knowing that You are eternal and unshakeable. In Jesus' name, Amen.

Prayers for Discipline and Self-Control

Prayer for Strength in Exercising Discipline

Scripture: "For God gave us a spirit not of fear but of power and love and self-control." 2 Timothy 1:7

Prayer: Heavenly Father, I thank You that You have given me a spirit of power, love, and self-control (2 Timothy 1:7). I ask for Your strength today to exercise discipline in every area of my life. Help me to make choices that align with Your will and grant me the self-control to resist temptations that would lead me astray. When my flesh wants to rebel, may Your Spirit rise within me, giving me the strength to overcome. Teach me to walk in the fruit of the Spirit and to be disciplined in my actions and thoughts. I place my trust in You, knowing that with Your help, I can live a life of self-control. In Jesus' name, Amen.

Prayer for Victory Over Temptation

Scripture: "No temptation has overtaken you that is not common to man. God is faithful, and He will not let you be tempted beyond your ability, but with the temptation He will also provide the way of escape, that you may be able to endure it." 1 Corinthians 10:13

Prayer: Father, I thank You for Your faithfulness in providing a way of escape from every temptation (1 Corinthians 10:13). I pray for Your guidance and strength when I face moments of temptation. Give me the wisdom to recognize the escape route You provide and the courage to take it. Lord, I ask that You strengthen my resolve to resist the urges of the flesh and to walk in Your righteousness. I claim victory over every temptation, knowing that You have already provided the way to overcome. I surrender my weaknesses to You, trusting in Your power to help me endure. In Jesus' name, Amen.

Prayer for Consistent Obedience and Discipline

Scripture: "But I discipline my body and keep it under control, lest after preaching to others I myself should be disqualified." 1 Corinthians 9:27

Prayer: Lord, I desire to live a disciplined life, to bring my body and mind into submission to Your will (1 Corinthians 9:27). Help me to remain consistent in my actions, thoughts, and words. May my discipline reflect Your character and lead others to You. I pray that I will not be swayed by the desires of the flesh but will keep my eyes focused on the prize of living a life pleasing to You. Empower me to maintain self-control in every area, from my diet to my thoughts, to my relationships and time management. May I always seek to glorify You through my discipline. In Jesus' name, Amen.

Prayer for Self-Control in the Face of Anger

Scripture: "Know this, my beloved brothers: let every person be quick to hear, slow to speak, slow to anger; for the anger of man does not produce the righteousness of God." James 1:19-20

Prayer: Father, I ask for Your help in practicing self-control, especially when it comes to my anger. Your Word reminds me to be quick to listen, slow to speak, and slow to anger (James 1:19-20). Lord, help me to control my emotions and not let anger rule over me. Teach me to respond with grace and patience, even in challenging situations. May my reactions be in alignment with Your righteousness, and may I reflect Your peace in every interaction. I ask for Your wisdom to recognize when I'm becoming angry and the self-discipline to choose a calm and loving response. In Jesus' name, Amen.

Prayer for Self-Control in Relationships

Scripture: "Let all bitterness and wrath and anger and clamor and slander be put away from you, along with all malice." Ephesians 4:31

Prayer: Lord, I pray that You would help me to exercise self-control in my relationships. I ask that all bitterness, wrath, anger, and malice be removed from my heart (Ephesians 4:31). Help me to love others as You have loved me, with patience, kindness, and forgiveness. May I not let negative emotions dictate my actions but rather walk in Your peace and love. Give me the strength to communicate with grace and to handle conflict with wisdom. I choose to release any anger or resentment that may hinder my relationships and allow Your love to flow freely. In Jesus' name, Amen.

Prayer for Self-Control Over Desires

Scripture: "So I do not run aimlessly; I do not box as one beating the air. But I discipline my body and keep it under control, lest after preaching to others I should be disqualified." 1 Corinthians 9:26-27

Prayer: Father, help me to have self-control over my desires, both physical and emotional. Your Word teaches me that I should not run aimlessly or be ruled by my impulses (1 Corinthians 9:26-27). Help me to keep my body under control and to live with purpose and focus. When I feel the pull of desires that are not of You, remind me of Your greater purpose for my life and give me the strength to resist. May I pursue holiness and self-discipline, honoring You with every choice I make. I trust that with Your strength, I can overcome any temptation. In Jesus' name, Amen.

Prayer for Self-Control in Words and Speech

Scripture: "Let your speech always be gracious, seasoned with salt, so that you may know how you ought to answer each person." Colossians 4:6

Prayer: Lord, I pray for discipline in my speech. Your Word tells me that my speech should always be gracious and seasoned with salt (Colossians 4:6). I ask that You give me the self-control to speak with kindness, respect, and wisdom in every conversation. Help me to hold my tongue when necessary and to use my words to build others up, not tear them down. I pray that my words would reflect Your love and truth. Let me be slow to speak and quick to listen, bringing peace and healing with every word. In Jesus' name, Amen.

Prayer for Self-Control in Times of Temptation

Scripture: "Submit yourselves therefore to God. Resist the devil, and he will flee from you." James 4:7

Prayer: Father, I submit myself to You and resist the enemy in the name of Jesus (James 4:7). I ask for Your help in moments of temptation when my flesh seeks to lead me away from Your will. Strengthen my spirit and give me the discipline to resist the devil and his lies. Help me to recognize temptation for what it is and to stand firm in Your Word. I trust that as I resist, the enemy will flee. Fill me with Your Spirit so that I can walk in victory and exercise self-control in all things. In Jesus' name, Amen.

Prayer for Spiritual Strength to Exercise Discipline

Scripture: "I can do all things through him who strengthens me." Philippians 4:13

Prayer: Lord, I thank You for the strength You give me to do all things through Christ, who strengthens me (Philippians 4:13). I ask You to empower me with the spiritual strength to live a disciplined life, one that honors You in everything I do. Whether it's in my habits, my thoughts, or my actions, help me to be disciplined and to keep my focus on You. I surrender all areas of weakness to You and trust that You will provide the strength I need to overcome. May my life reflect Your power, and may I walk in victory through Christ. In Jesus' name, Amen.

Prayer for Self-Control in Time Management

Scripture: "Look carefully then how you walk, not as unwise but as wise, making the best use of the time, because the days are evil." Ephesians 5:15-16

Prayer: Father, I ask for Your help in managing my time wisely. Your Word reminds me to make the best use of the time because the days are evil (Ephesians 5:15-16). Help me to stay disciplined and focused on the priorities You have set before me. Give me the self-control to avoid distractions and to use my time in ways that glorify You. I pray for the wisdom to organize my day, to stay diligent in my work, and to take time for rest and rejuvenation. Help me to honor You with how I spend every moment. In Jesus' name, Amen.

Special Acknowledgments

With gratitude, I would like to extend my appreciation to everyone who has played a role in making this journey possible. To the Supporters and Listeners, this project has been made possible by your participation, presence, and feedback. I am honored to have such incredible people by my side. I sincerely thank every one of you with special appreciation to my mother, all members on Patreon as well as YouTube, Sarah Bonesteel, Brina Denise, Lee Ann Flynn, Tasha Walker, and all the hosts who have graciously let me partake in their vision as well. Thank You.

www.ingramcontent.com/pod-product-compliance
Lightning Source LLC
Chambersburg PA
CBHW060504090426
42735CB00011B/2112

* 9 7 9 8 2 1 8 6 5 2 2 6 5 *